Digital School Teacher

The Ultimate Guide To Online Teaching

Trisha T. Mooring

from various sources. Please consult a licensed professional before attempting any techniques outlined in this book.

By reading this document, the reader agrees that under no circumstances is the author responsible for any losses, direct or indirect, that are incurred as a result of the use of the information contained within this document, including, but not limited to, errors, omissions, or inaccuracies.

Table of Contents

Introduction

The year 2020 will go down in history as the year that revolutionized teaching. Who would have known that with the beginning of the new decade, education would take place over Zoom or Microsoft Teams? While many teachers knew that at some point in the future technology would play a significant factor in teaching, no one anticipated that the transition from traditional teaching to online learning would have happened so soon. Nonetheless, these are the cards that we have been dealt and as teachers, it is our responsibility to make the necessary adaptation to online learning so that our students are just as enriched online as they were in our classrooms. Throughout this book, you will learn various strategies, tips, and suggestions to make your teaching experience online successful and engaging. You will learn how to create lessons that grab your students' attention and ensure that they are actively participating in every discussion.

A thought that may be going through your mind right now is "Am I qualified to be an online teacher?" As an educator myself, I understand how overwhelming it is to transition to online learning—and there are many reasons why you might be feeling like this. First of all, you are probably feeling like a beginner teacher all over again because you're not the most tech-savvy person you know. Online learning relies predominantly on digital tools and platforms for hosting and supporting online lessons. It can be embarrassing to admit that you are afraid or anxious about using many of the digital tools offered to improve your teaching experience online. However, you need to realize that no one is born knowing how to operate softwares and digital systems. It is a skill that is increasingly perfected over time and the more you willingly expose yourself to these tools, the greater your confidence will be in using them!

Another reason why you're probably overwhelmed is because you are not confident that you will be able to meet your students' needs through online teaching. Over the years, you may have attended many training conferences or seminars about how to empower your students in the classroom environment. If you have been teaching for many years now, I am certain that you know the in's and out's of connecting with your students, controlling order in the classroom, and creating a positive atmosphere around learning. However, now that classrooms have been closed and learning has been transferred online, you wonder how you will have the same amount of influence over your students as you did when you could teach face-to-face. You wonder whether you will be able to intuitively pick up on your students' needs, notice when students are disengaged, or positively impact your students like you used to. These are all valid concerns, especially because you are still trialing what works and doesn't when it comes to online teaching.

This book aims to improve your level of confidence teaching and planning your lessons online. Many teachers are out of their comfort zones, having to teach in ways that are foreign to what they are used to. Without a proper online learning strategy, teachers feel as though they are not offering their students as much value as they did before. The good news is that successful online learning strategies for both primary and secondary school teachers are available throughout the following chapters. You will learn how to setup your virtual classroom and all of the tools and platforms that will offer you convenience in teaching. You will also learn effective skills and tricks to command your students' attention and engage them in a powerful way. Your online lessons will feel intimate and enriched with knowledge and value. All of these useful strategies will save you time preparing for lessons, providing you with a healthier work-life balance. After all, digital technology is meant to take the strain out of the work and make your teaching a lot more convenient, right?

Well, this is what I learned when I began teaching online a few years ago. Fortunately, I was ahead of the movement to online learning because I offered tutoring lessons to an online audience. From as early as the year 2010, I was setting up tutoring lessons online and making worksheets and tests available at the click of a button. However, getting started wasn't a walk in the park. I was faced with a very sobering dilemma: How can I make my two decades of educational experience relevant to an online audience who may never have a physical interaction with me? How will I build a meaningful connection with them and ensure that they are gaining valuable knowledge from my lessons? While I was confident in my ability to command a classroom, online learning placed me in unfamiliar territory. Through many years of trial and error, as well as openly asking my students to give me feedback on the lessons, I finally came to a point where I was confident in delivering value for money online! I came to realize that technology was a gift that was available to enhance my teaching experience instead of hamper it.

The bond between student and teacher—which was my number one priority—was strengthened when I knew the strategies of how to use technology to create a continuous loop of information being transferred to and fro between myself and my students. What a relief it was for a seasoned teacher like myself to feel empowered to use technology in making my lessons more efficient. Since conquering my hesitancy with online learning, I have become passionate about sharing my experiences and knowledge regarding this topic to other educators who may be feeling anxious about this new wave of teaching. You can finally breathe a sigh of relief because in this book, I will address all of your fears and concerns, and ultimately give you the conviction that you need to become an influential online teacher!

"Tell me and I forget. Teach me and I remember.
Involve me and I learn."

~ Benjamin Franklin

Chapter One:

Getting Ready to Teach

Online

When I first began teaching students online, I had no idea how to adjust my teaching style to a virtual classroom. I remember during the early months of my teaching many children were dropping out like flies. I didn't understand why their interest was so short lived, considering that the knowledge I was giving them was of high quality. It was only after sending out a survey to all of my students (those who were enrolled in my classes and those who had dropped out) that I learned that I was the problem. I had ignorantly assumed that just because my lessons were now hosted online, the delivery of my classes didn't have to change. Oh boy was I mistaken! Students noted that my lessons were not engaging enough. I would spend an hour giving a lecture about a very relevant topic instead of breaking down my content into palatable information and using multiple options of interacting with my students.

My lengthy monologues were not appreciated, nor was the density of my lessons. Students wanted to be entertained and asked to actively participate in the lessons. They were unhappy with the passive role I had unknowingly assigned to them during lessons because it wasn't enriching their learning experience. Another error on my part was to upload large volumes of learning materials online with the expectation for my students to go through the resources and continue engaging with the topics. It took me a while to realize that my excessive content was in fact decreasing the level at which my students were absorbing new ideas and knowledge. While it was easier for me to hold my students' attention in a physical classroom, it was harder to grab their attention in a digital classroom due to the many distractions that they were faced with in their environment.

With this new insight and feedback, I was determined to learn how to be an anchor for my students' online learning experience and keep them grounded and engaged. I wanted my students to feel as though I was present with them in the room in order for them to feel supported. Therefore, a few things had to change. Firstly, I had to bid farewell to my old-school teaching methods and be open to learning newer ways of structuring and presenting my lessons online. I also had to be willing to consider different ways to interact with my students so that I could hold their attention for as long as possible. More than ever, I was more focused on sharing value rather than dictating principles and theories with my students. Armed with this new conviction, I was ready to provide valuable knowledge to a generation of tech-savvy students online!

The Four Common Challenges Experienced With Distance Learning

Unlike me, you have the opportunity to prepare in advance for your online teaching. Part of your preparation involves being aware of some of the challenges that come with distance learning. Remember that in most cases, your students are also new to the environment of a virtual classroom and so they will have to do a lot of adjusting and adapting too. The challenges presented in distance learning are specific to the process and format involved in online learning. For instance, you may have an issue of poor internet connectivity or students losing their concentration because of the events taking place in their homes, and so forth. I found that the more I took time to understand this new environment that I would be teaching in, I could create innovative solutions to combat some of these challenges. For instance, to help my students maintain their level of concentration throughout the lesson, I would give them breaks to grab a glass of water or stretch their legs. This would ensure that they are receiving enough stimulation throughout my lessons. Below are four common challenges that you will be presented with during your online teaching and some innovative solutions to combat them:

Number One: Feeling Isolated From Other Learners

Distance learning can be a lonely experience for you as the teacher as well as for your students who miss the interactions with their peers. The buzz of the classroom kept your students energized and engaged in lessons for a longer period of time. Now with nothing more than their PC or laptop to look at, your students may feel a sense of isolation which in turn discourages them from participating in lessons. Feeling isolated can also make your students less willing to participate in group discussions, exercises, or activities. I am sure that if you and your students had the choice, you would be back in the classroom feeding off of each other's energy. However, it is possible to recreate that same chemistry online.

Firstly, you can incorporate virtual group activities as part of your online curriculum. Allow your students to video conference each other and plan a group project or activity. This will give them an opportunity to socialize with each other, as well as to consolidate their learnings through the sharing of value and knowledge among group members. Secondly, I would encourage you to show your face during lessons instead of pointing the camera at the board or only offering audio. When students see your face (and hopefully you can see theirs) they feel as though you are directly speaking to them and this could encourage them to pay attention. Seeing your face will also remind them of the standards and expectations that you enforce in your classroom, bringing back a sense of normality in their new routine. Lastly, it is important for you to set up regular check-ins with each student in your class where you find out how they are coping with the workload or balancing home and school life. Enforcing this open line of communication will make your students feel supported in their academic life even though they are not physically at school.

Number Two: The Lack of Discipline in Learners

There is a level of regulation that a teacher feels in a physical classroom. You can readily enforce disciplinary measures, use your body language or tone of voice to send clear instructions, or read the energy of the students before adopting an alternative measure. In a physical classroom, you can easily pick up where you left off, assess the quality of the work presented by students at any time, and pick up on those students who are battling with understanding the content. This amount of structure and routine is a luxury that virtual classrooms don't come with. Even though you will have some students who are self-disciplined and can adhere strictly to deadlines, others may feel confused or anxious to complete tasks on their own without their teacher standing behind them.

As an online teacher, your goal should be to teach your students how to be responsible for their own work. Giving your students responsibility to start and finish their work according to your standards—and on time— is a necessary life skill for them to learn. It also means that you can rest assured knowing that your lessons flow as smoothly as they did in a physical classroom. Teaching students how to be self-disciplined begins with helping them set up a structure or routine that would facilitate their learnings. For instance, you would help your students create a timetable for their day. On the timetable you would designate time for online learning, completing homework, physical exercise or playing sports, and any other healthy activity that would give your students a sense of balance during the course of their day. Another way to enforce self-discipline in your students is to set clear and measurable goals for every task that you do. Clearly specify the time that your students have to complete the task, the measurable outcome, and efforts to reinforce accountability (this could include instructions on how to submit their work).

Number Three: Technical Difficulties Accessing Online Class

It would be unfair for us to assume that every child has the same access to technology in their communities or households. Not every student will have internet connectivity at home or the suitable technological device to use for online learning. This presents a challenge for you as the teacher because your aim is to reach and engage with all of your students in your virtual classroom. When some students are unable to join the lesson, it may also mean that you as the teacher have to find an alternative way to reach these students and communicate the information similarly to how it was shared in your online lesson. Another challenge regarding technology is that as much as we call young people "digital natives," there are many of them who are technologically illiterate.

This means that they struggle to operate technology or follow instructions online. They may be reluctant to use a teaching software because of their fears of getting stuck. To ensure that your students are all on the same page regarding access and familiarity with technology, it is important for you as the educator to make sure that your students have access to all of the technology that they need throughout your lessons. For those who do not have access, an alternative plan must be arranged so that they are able to receive the same knowledge and skills that were shared with the online class. For example, you can plan your online lessons in advance and deliver a written document and audio file to the students without access to the internet. They would then have the opportunity to read over the material with a caregiver, and listen to your audio files in order to fully grasp the concepts. When familiarizing those students who have access to technology with the various teaching platforms, host frequent tutorials or sessions where you show students and their caregivers how to use the various digital tools.

Number Four: Struggling to Adapt

The switch from a traditional classroom to a virtual one can be a challenge for both educator and learner. This challenge is heightened when either you or the student are resistant to this new change. The truth of the matter is that online learning will require you to learn online systems and tools for enhancing the experience of the virtual classroom. Most times, when the teacher is onboard and willing to make the necessary adjustments to their teaching style, the students display more confidence in the new way of learning. In other words, many times a student's unwillingness to embrace online learning is modelled by the teacher's unwillingness to embrace the full experience of going digital. When you as the teacher find it difficult to remain disciplined in setting and following the new online learning routine, your students will also lose accountability.

I know how overwhelmed you must be feeling, having been stripped of your traditional classroom environment; however, your students are depending on you to set the tone and culture for their online learning experience. Your students need you now more than ever to fuel their online lessons with excitement and make them feel empowered to take responsibility for their learnings. One of the ways that you can help students who are struggling to adapt to the new virtual classroom is by discussing the benefits of online learning and ways of enhancing their learning experience at home. Sometimes the fear or resistance to online learning is a result of limited information about it. Regularly hold open discussions where you encourage your students to share their experiences with online learning and the challenges that they may be facing. Find ways to resolve their concerns, silence their fears, and offer support whenever it is needed.

Preparing for Online Teaching: Handy Tips and Suggestions

Online teaching can be a daunting process, especially for those educators who have reservations about relying on technology for effective lesson delivery. The adjustment between a physical classroom and a virtual one is also one that takes time to get used to. Nevertheless, the migration to digital platforms does not mean that the quality of your lessons will be lessened in any way. If anything, integrating technological tools within your lessons can provide your students with a more enriching learning experience. I always suggest that teachers first develop the content that they would like to share with their students, and thereafter plan ways of integrating online tools to make the lesson more engaging and interactive with their students. While it is impossible for you to replicate the experience of teaching in a physical classroom, encouraging students to interact in virtual group discussion or team projects can imitate the feeling of being together in a collaborative environment. This will motivate your students to continue participating in lessons and reaching out to their peers for assistance with learning material.

When preparing for online teaching, it is also important to imagine the entire online learning experience from the perspective of your students. It is common for teachers to plan and structure online lessons from a purely academic perspective and forget to consider the people who will be absorbing all of this dense information. While it is important to follow your institution's curriculum and complete all of the learning outcomes for a module, online teachers have the extra responsibility of ensuring that their lessons have an X Factor or entertainment value associated with them. For example, you need to consider the variety of media tools that your students are already familiar with and incorporate them in your lessons. This will make your lessons more student-centered and thus encourage them to continue attending your classes. Ask yourself: What are the ways that I can make my online lessons stimulating for my students? Answering this question requires you to find ways of using media tools creatively in order to encourage interaction. For instance, you might ask your students to create a podcast or video interview as one of their homework assignments so that they can stimulate their minds differently as opposed to a written assignment.

Below are more tips and suggestions that will help you prepare for your online teaching journey:

Perhaps the most important piece of advice that I would give an educator preparing to teach online is to ensure that they have the necessary training to teach online. In other words, they need to be familiar with the expectations that come with online learning and setting up a virtual classroom. When I began teaching online, I made the assumption that my 20 years plus of teaching in a traditional classroom would be sufficient training and experience to teach. While I was an effective face-to-face teacher, I hadn't acquired the skills to effectively teach students online. For example, I needed to learn how to operate technological devices and tools including microphones, webcams, and other video features. I also needed to learn how to combine a variety of media during my lessons in order to enhance my students' learning experience. Another skill that I needed to learn was how to communicate my messages in a way that wouldn't cause misinterpretations.

For some of my lessons, video wasn't an option and I relied solely on audio recordings and text-chatting discussion boards to relay important instructions to my students. As a result of the limited visual or face-to-face communication, my messages ran the risk of being misunderstood or misinterpreted. Therefore, I needed to learn how to effectively communicate with my students in the absence of non-verbal cues like my body language or facial expressions. My audio or written communication had to provide students with enough depth and breadth for them to carry out instructions with confidence. This is why I place emphasis on the importance of receiving the necessary training before you can start teaching students online. Part of your training may be watching YouTube videos about setting up a virtual classroom and how to utilize all of the features on your technological devices so that you can create an all-encompassing classroom feeling.

The second tip is to set realistic expectations and collaborate as much as possible with other online educators. As a teacher, you want to offer your students as much value virtually as they would receive in a physical classroom. However, be kind to yourself when you begin your online teaching by keeping your expectations low. This is new territory for you and there is still a lot of on-the-job training that you will learn. Therefore, if you experience technical difficulties during a lesson or decide on using only one media tool in the beginning, just breathe and realize that you are doing a great job! As you become more familiar with online teaching, you will learn how to make your processes more efficient and apply new techniques and tools to your lessons. It is also just as important to have a network of support as you begin online teaching. Setup a weekly Zoom or Skype meeting with other online teachers and create an agenda that allows the group to share ideas that they have sampled and their online teaching experience on that particular week. It would be helpful if you or the administrator of the meeting records all of the weekly sessions and have these video footages available on a shared online folder (try using Google Docs or Dropbox).

If you do not have access to a network of teachers in your community, you can find the necessary support for online teaching in online communities. For instance, "Teacher Tube" is an amazing online community that allows educators or professionals to share instructional videos. Members of the community are given the privilege of watching, rating, and starting discussions around the content. A community such as this one can help you learn how to present information in an innovative and engaging way to your students. Another supportive online community that you can look into is "Teach Ade." This educator-centered community allows educators to connect with each other, start or join groups based on their interests, and share resources, links, lesson plans, and other teaching material. If you are an educator familiar with social media, you can follow the hashtags #FFBWEDNESDAY, #TINYVOICETUESDAY and #PLANNINGSHOUTOUT on Twitter. Do you also have a Facebook account? You can follow the following Facebook groups: "Teach With Tech," "Teachers Ask Teachers," and "Teaching Ideas."

The third tip is to rehearse your lesson structure and virtual classroom experience before the actual lesson takes place. Rehearsing your lessons prior to the actual event will allow you to test technological equipment and tools to see how well they work individually and when combined in a smooth transition between tools. You can rehearse your lessons with another educator or ask a family member at home to stand in place of the student while you conduct the necessary testing. One crucial element which you need to test is the speaking activities. How many times have you been on a video call with a friend and the audio didn't pick up? Perhaps too many times to count. Testing the quality of your audio before the online lesson will help you prevent any hiccups or awkward moments during your live or recorded event. When testing audio function, practice muting the microphones of the other parties and allowing one person to speak at a time. Furthermore, test the "raising hands" function, writing in the given chat box, and using breakout rooms. Of course, depending on your chosen platform, these functions may or may not be available. Therefore, play around with what your platform offers you and see how well it compliments your lesson structure.

The fourth tip is to plan your lessons well in advance. In a virtual classroom, your students are not anywhere near you and at times, they may be in a different time zone than you. Thus, your online lessons need to be well coordinated and planned to ensure that you have considered all of your students and their online learning experience. In a virtual classroom you cannot "wing it" because your online students will need more academic support and educational material than what your classroom students needed. Therefore I would suggest that you have a syllabus planned out before you record or go live with your first online lesson. Ensure that you have created all of the written, audio, and video content to go along with each lesson. Sometimes, early preparation of content can help you plan how each lesson will continue after the next and build up of concepts and topics. Furthermore, preparing content in advance allows you to upload your full syllabus online and give students the opportunity to go through the course or module and familiarize themselves in advance with the discussions that you will have together. They will also feel less anxious about taking the course or module because they have access to the syllabus and therefore understand the expectations required of them.

Once you have planned your syllabus, it is important for you to familiarize yourself with various technological tools. Many people find technology to be intimidating because of the intricacies involved with some innovations. However, did you know that there are softwares and platforms that are beginner-friendly, offering you online tutorials and live customer support whenever you need it? The greatest myth about technology is that you need to be a Mark Zuckerberg to confidently use it. Anyone with any level of technological competency can learn how to become a pro with technology. When preparing to teach online, you will first need to invest in the best and most reliable (according to your budget) equipment and software. Three standard things that you will need before you start is a computer or laptop, a fast and reliable internet connection, and the most convenient and feature-rich online software. Take your time when choosing the best hardware and software; ask other online teachers for their advice, and choose software that will meet all of your classroom needs.

The final tip is to make sure that you set up your film set or work station in an adequate working environment. Working remotely will be a new experience for many teachers who are accustomed to a traditional classroom environment where you have a decent amount of space to walk around, write on the board, and engage with every student in the class. In order to make the most out of working remotely, you need to create an encouraging and fully-equipped workspace. Setting up your workspace on the kitchen counter is not encouraging. The location of your workspace needs to be in a space that is designated exclusively for recording your lessons or hosting live events. This space should be full of natural light, inspiring for you and the viewer, and encourage productivity. Therefore it goes without saying that this space must be free of any distractions such as a TV playing in the background or the sound of cars or family members. It is important to note that while a visually appealing space will capture the attention of your students, you must also be comfortable in that space and have all of your physical needs met and supported. For instance, purchase an ergonomic chair, bring a glass of water, and any other personal comforts which won't be a distraction to you or your students.

Chapter Two:

Lesson Creation for Online and Blended Environments

The educational material that students receive during online learning is the first glimpse that they get into what the module or course is about. They have an opportunity to look through what topics and activities they will be partaking in for the weeks to follow and get a general sense of the knowledge that they will acquire once the module or course has come to completion. To the educator, the online content shared with students forms the backbone or framework of the work that will be covered during lessons. This framework allows online teachers to get a sense of what they will teach each lesson and how much work they need to cover. Without this framework, online lessons lose direction and become disorganized. Therefore it is to the benefit of both teacher and student that online lessons have an introduction, clarifying aspects, and all of the supporting elements that will make each lesson flow into the next effortlessly.

When planning and developing an online lesson, it is important for educators to consider three elements, namely the presentation, structure, and content of the online lesson. Paying attention to these three elements will ensure that educators deliver a lesson that is well-coordinated and provides the student with as much information as possible. When a student accesses their lesson material, they should be able to look through it and within a few minutes have a firm understanding of what the lesson will be about and the expectations from the educator. One of the ways to achieve this amount of transparency and clear-cut communication is to first have a full picture of the lesson framework before you start writing any content or collecting any material. Think about what you intend for your students to grasp from this lesson, as well as the learning aims and outcomes that you would like students to gain. It is also worth thinking about how you plan on assessing the skills and knowledge that students have gained throughout the lesson or how to consolidate everything that was learned. All of these considerations will significantly impact the structure and style of your lesson.

Depending on your intended learning outcomes and the general approach you want to take for your lessons, you will select the most appropriate lesson structure. For example, if you intend on sharing large quantities of text (similar to an e-book or online slideshows), you would select media tools that accommodate for large volumes of text and your main task would be finding the best way to split the text into manageable portions. When you intend on introducing various concepts to your students and give a general commentary of each, your lessons wouldn't be saturated with long texts. However, you would need to structure your lessons in a way that allows you to include a variety of links, sources, and activities that would break down the material and help your students flow through each concept or idea introduced to them. When your lesson is based on problem-solving, reflections, or looking at case studies, you will find that there is less structure needed during the lessons. However, you would still need to include clear instructions and lesson objectives to help your students structure their independent or collaborative work.

Regardless of the structure that your online lesson takes, there is a basic structure that all online lessons should include to help students navigate through the lesson, module, or course with minimal confusion or misunderstandings. Firstly, you will need to break your lesson content into bit-sized sections either by length, the duration of each segment, or the various topics that will be discussed. If you choose to split the content by duration, ensure that each section does not exceed two hours, which is generally the maximum amount of time for each learning block. Secondly, you will need to provide clear yet descriptive headings for each section, topic, or sub-topic. This will help to organize your lesson while also allowing your students to plan on which sections they will like to work on in each online teaching session. Lastly, it is important for you to add an introduction and summary of each section at the beginning and at the end. This will give your students an overview of what is to come, the learning outcomes, and time allocated to complete the section. It will also provide a summary of all of the key points and themes that were mentioned in the lesson.

How to Plan an Online Teaching Lesson

Planning your online lessons in advance will ensure that you have a clear understanding of the flow and structure of your lessons and how to effectively bring your message across. By preparing your online lessons, you will also avoid any content repetition or incorporating content that does not compliment the overall purpose of the lesson. Since it is difficult to "wing" an online teaching session, preparing your lessons in advance will give you the necessary time to plan how you intend on delivering the content in the most engaging way to your students. For example, after having a look through your content you might find an opportunity to add a quick quiz or game that would add value to the learning process. Fortunately for you, the internet is full of templates which do all of the hard work of structuring your online lesson for you! These templates are designed to tick all of the necessary boxes that make an online lesson impactful and full of value for your students. These templates are also particularly useful for teachers who need a bit more inspiration or direction in designing their online lessons. To start you off, you can visit "Education dot com" (https://www.education.com/lesson-plans/), and "Share my lesson dot com" (https://sharemylesson.com/) for lesson plan ideas and downloads.

As teachers, we can sometimes underestimate the importance of setting up a structure for our lessons, especially when we have taught the subject or module so many times that we don't need a framework for assistance. However, online lessons are time sensitive which means that within an hour or so, you should have covered all of the learning outcomes that you had planned to teach for that particular lesson. In a classroom environment, work that is not covered within the lesson time is usually carried over to the following day and time is restructured accordingly. While it is possible to have virtual lessons that continue over several videos, using this kind of strategy to plan your lessons may cause your students to skip videos or lose interest mid-way. Remember that your aim is to hold your students attention for as long as possible and thus, every lesson must offer something different, entertaining, and interesting.

When I speak to online teachers about structuring their online lessons, I tend to emphasize creativity over other technicalities. Looking at a screen for an hour or so is the most passive kind of learning anyone can do. After a few minutes of sitting on a chair, quietly listening to your calming voice, your students may become disengaged or feel rather sleepy. Since it is impossible to regulate their levels of concentration through a PC monitor, the content of your lesson will need to encourage your students' participation and action. Besides helping to keep your students focused, creative content makes learning and grasping new concepts easier. During your planning stage, take some time to think like your students and ask yourself: What would my students perceive as valuable content? What are their interests, ambitions, and dreams? What are some of their challenges, worries, and fears? Thinking like your students will help you come up with innovative ideas about topics to cover during lessons or incorporate various styles of delivering lessons to students.

Some simple tips for designing creative content include incorporating activities in your lessons that are out of the ordinary or spark your students' imagination. When organizing these activities in your lessons, ensure that similar activities are not grouped close to one another. There should always be enough variation and intrigue when planning and organizing your activities. Another tip is to use exercises as a continuation of learning. As much as exercises are designed to be fun, many times they become a missed opportunity to provide a practical demonstration of the concepts or ideas shared. Your exercises should consolidate the information learned during the lesson or test how well your students have understood the knowledge shared. It is also important to make time for questions or open discussions at the end of each lesson. When your online lessons are not taking place in real-time, you can encourage your students to answer a question and post it on the open discussion board of your course or module page. When your students engage with the content in this manner, it will help deepen their understanding of the shared ideas and concepts, as well as to learn from the responses of their peers.

Once you have planned your general framework and the creative content that you will include, you can then start thinking about which digital formats you will use from your virtual classroom toolbox. Online teachers who are new to the virtual classroom can use the most obvious and easiest formats at the beginning of their journey, and gradually work their way up to using more advanced formats and features. The benefit of using even the simplest digital format is that it improves the quality and value of your lesson, and allows you to expose your students to activities and features they would not find in a traditional classroom. For beginners, you can start by incorporating short videos into your lessons. You have the option of adding the video links or playing the full video during your lesson. Videos can be a great way to introduce primary resources such as interviews, documentaries, and other first-person narratives. They can also be useful in providing context about a topic before you begin teaching it to your students, giving them an entertaining introduction to the lesson.

Online teachers can also use images within their lessons to add some vibrancy. Images are a simple yet effective way of adding fun into your lessons. For instance, you can use images for a matching game, asking your students to match images that carry the same theme or message. You can also use images as a way to help your students visualize an idea. For instance, one of your activities could involve asking your students to find images on the internet which address or carry the same message as the concepts or ideas that you had discussed during the lesson. This activity would require students to review their learnings and actively search for appropriate images that validate what concepts or ideas they have learned. It can also be fun for students to see what kind of images their classmates were able to find! Other forms of images that provide an educational benefit include diagrams and infographics. Adding these to your lesson will provide a much needed break from heavy text and allow your students to learn through pictures.

Another creative tip is to use color in your lessons as a way to encourage learning. Color coding is a creative tool that teachers can always use to encourage engagement from their students. Color works at a subconscious level, sending information to the brain and influencing your students' behavior positively. Color coding your virtual classroom will help you create an environment conducive of learning and enhance your students' levels of productivity. For example, using different colors can help students distinguish between two concepts and ideas or to compare and contrast information. Color coding can also be used to highlight the most important points or phrases in text, helping students organize and deepen their understanding of the information. While using color can enrich learning, too much of it has the opposite effect. It can overcomplicate concepts or cause information to look the same. Therefore, the general rule of thumb is to stick to two or three colors throughout the lesson and use them for specific purposes. For example, you would use blue to highlight main ideas and orange to indicate additional information.

Components of a Good Online Lesson

When creating an online lesson, the traditional elements of a handout, wordy Powerpoint presentation, or questionnaire won't help you create enough value that you can share with your students. In order for your online lesson to be of high quality and effective, you must pay attention to the design and the treatment of the content. Making the migration from traditional to virtual classroom requires you to make time for strategic planning and adaptation of content so that you can achieve the best results. While every online lesson will take on a different style or layout, every successful online lesson includes certain components that enhance its value and keep students engaged throughout. First and foremost, great online lessons have a well-defined format which guides how the lessons are structured and presented. There are three main formats that online lessons can take, namely asynchronous, synchronous, and hybrid learning.

Lessons structured around asynchronous learning allow the student to engage directly with the content and the interaction with the teacher is usually through pre-recorded videos or audio. Other forms of communicating with the teacher are through emails, discussion boards, or forums where teachers can answer questions that students may have or provide additional learning material. The main benefit of this kind of format is that it offers the student greater flexibility in deciding the best time to complete the lesson and at what pace they follow. The second format is synchronous learning where the online lesson takes place in real-time. During the Coronavirus pandemic, many schools across the country adopted this type of format for online teaching, hosting online classes in real-time and mimicking the normal school timetable. The lessons are usually delivered through video conferencing with learners, real-time discussions, or sharing audio. The benefit of using this format is that students feel supported going through the content with the teacher as opposed to tackling it in their own time. Both teachers and students also have an opportunity to share knowledge and clarify misunderstandings by the constant dialogue back and forth.

The third format for online lessons is hybrid learning where features of asynchronous and synchronous learning are utilized. For instance, the lesson may begin with a real-time interaction between teacher and student and thereafter, the student has an opportunity to complete homework or extra readings on their own. This approach gives students the chance to learn concepts and ideas through teacher interaction and then consolidate their learnings at their own pace and in their own time. Therefore, the hybrid learning approach provides students with a thorough form of teaching while also making them responsible for their own work. When choosing which format to use, think about the students that you are teaching and which format would support their needs the most. Secondary school students would benefit more from a hybrid learning format while college students would prefer an asynchronous learning approach.

When you have chosen a format for your online lessons, it will become easier to see the adaptations you need to make to your content in order to meet the needs of your students. The next component of a good online lesson involves the instructional design that is included. No matter how well your content was received in your classroom or how visually appealing it was on your projector, it must undergo a redesign in order to have the same powerful effect in your virtual classroom. The visual design of your online lesson is an important element to keep your students engaged; however, it is also a valuable tool to assist your students in the learning process. Incorporating beautiful images or insightful videos is not enough to make your teaching material effective—you are required to go a step further and learn how the human brain processes information. Psychologists study the five multimedia principles that can enrich online learning and reduce the cognitive discomfort typically caused by the incorrect combination of text, images, videos, and other media elements.

The principle of coherency states that all components of an online lesson including the topics, themes, and learning objects must flow and compliment each other continuously throughout the lesson. This encourages students to pick up on similarities and differences between content effortlessly and form solid arguments and conclusions. This also implies that any content or theme that does not add any value to the student's learning process must be excluded. The principle of signalling states that significant elements of the online lesson must be emphasized using visual or vocal resources so that the student's focus can be directed toward them. This also implies that elements that are not as important should not have as much emphasis placed on them. Since your students cannot focus on every minute detail, choose a few main points, themes, or ideas that you want to highlight and use visual tools such as infographics, video, or audio to help them stand out.

The principle of redundancy states that it is better for online teachers to use a combination of audio and graphics as opposed to using a combination of audio and text in their online lessons because the latter causes cognitive overload in the student's mind. Audio and graphics are complementary to one another and both offer an experience that is unique, while audio and text offer a similar experience and can lead to a saturation of information. The principle of spatial contiguity states that all of the descriptive information displayed on graphics or images should remain closely aligned with the written or audio content that is supplied alongside it. This would help the student pick up on patterns and deepen their comprehension of the content. The fifth and final principle of multimedia is the principle of temporal contiguity. This principle states that visual and auditory content should not be presented in an online lesson successively but simultaneously. This helps students draw parallels between the two formats and assist them in making connections or drawing conclusions about the various contents.

These five multimedia principles should be applied along with the following five design principles so that you are able to produce the most impactful online lesson possible! Using these five design principles gives you an opportunity to develop online lessons that are harmonious, have a powerful visual identity, and that are easy for your students to understand and memorize. The principle of alignment states that similar items need to be grouped in a linear fashion so that students can draw a visual connection when looking at them. You can align your content by designing it using a grid format. The invisible grid will give you a sense of structure and direction regarding how and where to place content. It will also help you achieve visual consistency throughout your lesson, especially when you are developing a large document. The principle of balance states that items should be grouped together at strategic points so that a balanced look and feel can be achieved. You may find that it looks more appealing to first present a topic, follow with examples, and then proceed to insert clickable links for further reading and comprehension. Continuing the same grouping of content throughout your lesson will help you achieve and maintain this balance.

The principle of consistency is similar to the principle of balance. This principle states that the main elements of your layout should be standardized and presented in the same manner consistently throughout your lesson. This will help you create a cohesive and harmonious visual identity and make it easier for your students to memorize work. The principle of contrast states that contrasting elements can be grouped together to create more of a visual impact when students glance over them and emphasize the main point or message of the content. When grouping contrasting elements together, you are allowing your students to connect the dots in their minds and learn by actively engaging with the content. The fifth and final principle of design is the principle of proximity. This principle states that grouping similar or related elements together can be powerful in helping your students draw similarities and connections between related content. This would serve to emphasize themes, ideas, or points already made which ultimately makes recognizing and memorizing the content much easier for your students.

The principles of multimedia and design are priceless tools that—when used correctly—will instantaneously enhance the learning experience and visual appeal of your online lesson and help you in making your content memorable. These principles also give you the creative freedom to differentiate your online lessons from others already discoverable on the internet, as well as to put your own unique elements that help to make your modules or courses stand out from the rest. These principles give you a creative license in the way you design your lessons and test the various ways that you can make the learning experience more engaging for your students.

Another component in creating an impactful online lesson is to consider the various scenarios and opportunities that you will have to interact with your students. Intentionally thinking about each scenario will help you plan ways of offering value throughout each interaction that is made and therefore keep your students engaged. The first interaction to consider is the one between students. The student-to-student interaction occurs during the lesson or course with or without the involvement or participation of the teacher or instructor. Generally, this kind of interaction takes place in chat boxes, forums, or on discussion boards. It is valuable for the overall success of the lesson because during these interactions, knowledge and ideas are exchanged and information is consolidated. You can encourage student-to-student interaction by incorporating group activities or making it a compulsory part of your lesson for students to answer or give feedback on a question or topic discussed during the lesson in the chat box or comments section.

The second interaction to consider is the one between you and your students. During these kinds of interactions, you are no longer just an educator or lecturer; instead you become a mentor or coach who offers guidance and support. You take on a more active role in ensuring that your students understand the content that you are sharing with them and that they are coping with the pace and complexity of the lesson. You can facilitate this kind of interaction through video conferencing, email exchange, or during online chat. While teachers can interact with a whole group or class of students, it can also be valuable to offer one-on-one check-ins and feedback sessions where you speak to individual students directly. The third and final interaction that you must consider when planning your online lesson is the interaction between the student and the content. This interaction happens when the student first enrolls in your classes and when they are engaging directly with the learning material. This kind of interaction is valuable because it gives your students a chance to read through the content at their own pace and formulate their own ideas, arguments, and conclusions. Using the five principles of multimedia and design will help you make your student's interaction with the content more efficient and full of value.

Four Steps to Create Your Own Lesson Plan

Those of you who wish to design your own templates for your online lessons can follow four simple steps in creating a winning lesson plan. The first step is the warm-up where you have an opportunity to engage with your students for the first time before starting the lesson. During this stage, you should refresh your students' minds by recapping knowledge learned from prior lessons and drawing the necessary links that you need to in order to place your current lesson in context. The warm-up stage will give your students a brief idea of what is to come and the learning outcomes that they will have achieved once the lesson is complete. Get your students' minds thinking about the topics that you will introduce later on in the lesson and have them apply their existing knowledge right away. One way of activating their minds is to play a quick game, make your students take a short quiz, or facilitate a reflection exercise. It is important for you to remember that your warm-up should make your students excited about engaging with the content that will follow. Keep your activities fun, light-hearted, and encouraging so that your students are looking forward to proceeding with the lesson.

The second step is where you would explain the content in the most easy-to-follow and stimulating manner possible. During this stage, you will have the opportunity to introduce your students to the learning material and present the overall argument or purpose of the lesson. If there are some pertinent themes and ideas that you would like to introduce, make sure that you explain them in detail and present them in the most memorable way. Depending on how advanced your students are, you can also include links to additional readings and resources that would help them develop a firm understanding of these themes and ideas. During the explanation stage, you will also have the opportunity to draw connections between various content as well as to help your students distinguish the differences between various content. By the end of this stage, they should be confident enough to perform an activity or exercise where the main themes or concepts can be assessed.

The third step involves elaborating on the content that was presented in the previous step. At this stage, the teacher is no longer presenting new information; rather they are guiding their students in consolidating the information already presented. This is where you give your students an opportunity to discuss and explore the learning material with you and ask clarifying questions. During this stage, you should encourage your students to do most of the speaking and offer assistance when you see that they are struggling to articulate themselves effectively. This is also the stage where you as the educator will gain an understanding of whether or not your students have understood the content that was explained to them. Some of the activities that you can facilitate during the elaboration stage include hosting a live chat where you ask your students questions about the content and have them provide answers. Another great idea would be to watch a video or read a passage pertaining to the work that was covered and allow your students to discuss what they watched or read and how it relates to the content.

The fourth and final step involved in planning your online lesson is to open up the floor for your students to elaborate on what they have learned. Once again, this stage should be fun, light-hearted, and encourage your students to partake in the next lesson or course that you have on offer. It can also be a very rewarding experience to hear what your students have learned and the ways that they have grown or have been enriched by the content. During this stage, you will ask your students to give their feedback on the lesson, as well as to ask follow-up questions or request one-on-one time with you. It is advised that you keep this stage unstructured so that you can allow your students to guide how this time is spent and the value that is created.

Chapter Three:

Best Tech Tools to Support

Online Learning

Before we can take a look at some online teaching strategies and practices, it is essential for us to discuss some of the popular technological solutions in the market today to help you on your online teaching journey. If you run a quick Google search, you will find thousands of products and services that offer simple to advanced features to help you setup your virtual classroom. The endless options make it difficult for teachers to select the most appropriate technological tools and softwares for their needs. Below is a list of apps and tools that I have personally curated for you that will help you make the best decisions regarding which tools and apps you will use as part of your virtual technological toolbox.

Lesson Planning Tools and Apps

Common Curriculum is a great website for beginner teachers that offers comprehensive lesson planning. It is suitable for students between pre-kindergarten and twelfth grade. It was designed to offer educators a lot of flexibility in developing their lessons, as well as to help teachers save and re-use as much of their content weekly, monthly, or yearly. One of the great features of this lesson planning tool is how it allows teachers to simply drag and drop lesson material for the week and adapt lessons whenever it is necessary. Common Curriculum also offers weekly, monthly, and yearly templates which provide the necessary framework for teachers so that they don't have to start from scratch with every module. This tool is especially useful for teachers who do not have available lesson planning tools in their schools or for those who do not have a lot of time to spare planning lessons. The tool is available through any browser using a desktop computer, laptop, or mobile device. It also allows you to make your lesson plans accessible to other colleagues, parents, and students who may want to go through the lesson plan, homework, classwork, and other learning resources that you have made available.

The only drawback with using Common Curriculum is that it doesn't offer multiple lesson planning per subject or course during a particular time frame. For example, Common Curriculum does not have features catering to advanced teachers who offer various online teaching courses per week and seek to schedule all of their lessons on one schedule. The built-in features on the website cater more so to teachers that teach the same subject on a continuous basis stretching over weeks or years. However, teachers may still be drawn to using this tool based on how affordable it is to use. Common Curriculum comes with a free 30-day trial and thereafter, teachers can opt for the free basic plan which provides standard features like free lesson planning, posting completed lessons to Google Classrooms, and printing or downloading plans. The paid pro plan goes for between $4.89 to $6.99 per month and it allows teachers to plan an entire unit or module. Schools and institutions can also purchase the schools plan at $90 per year, per teacher that helps school teachers organize all of their planbooks in one place and collaborate in teams.

Planboard is a lesson planning app that is free for individuals and teachers. It is suitable for students between kindergarten and twelfth grade. To access this app, you can download it on your Android or iOS device. The main purpose of this app is to help teachers plan lessons on the go and reduce overall classroom prep time. Some of the features available on Planboard include the ability to create content for lessons, create your own or assign lesson plan templates, create your own learning unit, assign standards to a lesson plan, track the progress and development of your curriculum, and so much more! On Planboard, teachers are also given the opportunity to share their lesson plans with their colleagues, substitute teachers, parents, and the students that they teach. Once you have successfully created a lesson, you have the option of printing the plan as a PDF document or sharing it digitally by using a custom link or embedding this custom link on other websites, making it easier for others to access the plan. The only drawback with using Planboard is that it does not offer pre-made templates and therefore teachers must create their own templates which can take some time to set up and organize.

Another great lesson planning website tool is Tes Teach with Blendspace. It is suitable for students between third grade and twelfth grade. This convenient multimedia lesson planning platform is easily accessible through their website and their Chrome or iPad app. Similarly to Common Curriculum, this tool offers teachers a drag and drop option to create and plan lesson content. Teachers can also drag and drop videos, images, text, spreadsheets, quizzes, and other out-of-the-box learning resources to make the learning experience more engaging. Teachers can upload content from just about anywhere on the internet including YouTube, Google, or from their personal cloud devices and computers. To access lesson plans, students are required to use a join code or alternatively, teachers can embed links to the lesson plans on other websites. Teachers can use a free Tes Teach with Blendspace account to design linear lessons that guide students through basic content.

For example, if you were a middle school biology teacher, you could share a lesson about the structure of a plant and incorporate links, videos, and quizzes to help your biology students build their understanding. You could also prepare pre-test assessments or create additional presentations to compliment your lessons. The benefit of using this tool—besides the fact that it is free—is that it offers teachers an appealing lesson plan design and that it works well on any technological device with internet connectivity. The only drawback found about this tool is that it offers very limited interaction between teacher and student. Unlike the other lesson planning tools, this one doesn't provide as much collaboration in lesson planning, even though it does come with a discussion box that both teachers and students can use to communicate to one another.

Multimedia Presentation and Interactive Activity Creation Tools for Teachers

Socrative is an interactive website that collects student responses to polls, quizzes, and other assessments. It is suitable for students between third grade and twelfth grade. The website is also available as an app for Android and iOS devices, helping students access and answer questions on the go. This platform helps teachers enhance the learning experience of students by incorporating user-created polls and quizzes. Once a teacher has designed and published a poll, students can immediately access it through a Room code. The answers to the poll would reflect on the teacher's dashboard and update every time a student submits their answers. When all of the students have responded to the poll, the teacher can reveal the summary of results and encourage students to have a discussion around it.

Teachers who are interested in storing the data collected can download an excel spreadsheet with all of the results. The only downside about Socrative is that it doesn't offer comprehensive analytical tools and therefore if you as a teacher seek to analyze a student's data over time, it will be time-consuming. Nonetheless, the price of this platform is a great incentive for teachers. The free version of the site includes up to fifty students per session and one public room. The pro version will cost you sixty dollars per year and it includes up to twenty public rooms and up to twenty activities published at one time.

One of the best multimedia presentation tools for online teachers and students is Prezi. It is suitable for students between sixth grade and twelfth grade. This tool allows both teachers and students to become storytellers by designing innovative presentations. On Prezi, users have the flexibility to design non-linear presentations and incorporate other multimedia elements from Flickr photos, YouTube, Twitter, Vimeo, and other media stored on their personal devices or cloud. Teachers who are looking for a more exciting alternative to the traditional Powerpoint presentation will find Prezi quite refreshing. Instead of presenting the information in an outline format, Prezi organizes information in a concept map and allows the presenter to toggle between topics, zooming in and out on the most relevant information. The basic plan offered by Prezi is free, however, it has very limited presenter features. The standard plan valued at three dollars per month offers users unlimited visual content and an online editing tool included. The only drawback with using Prezi is that its zoom feature can reduce the design quality of the presentation or become a distraction to some viewers. Moreover, designing your presentation with Prezi can be restricting, especially on the basic plan where there are limited colors, fonts, and shapes to choose from.

Infographics have become a powerful educational tool to simplify information and present it in the most appealing way. Infographics can help you relay facts, figures, and statistics by illustrating them graphically and drawing the necessary connections between data. Encouraging your students to create their own infographics can help them foster good research and data analysis skills. One of the best online tools available to create infographics is Easelly. It is suitable for students between seventh grade and twelfth grade. On an Easelly free account, students and teachers have access to hundreds of infographic templates which they can customize accordingly. Completed infographics can be downloaded onto one's computer or shared digitally. Teachers who are interested in using Easelly as part of their lesson plans can purchase the individual plan at four dollars per month and receive access to thirty free student accounts along with their plan. The only drawback about Easelly is that its free account offers very limited features and doesn't allow teachers access to view or supervise their students' progress.

Another great skill for your students to learn is how to edit videos. Animoto is an exciting video creation tool that students can use to create video slideshow presentations. It is suitable for students between seventh grade and twelfth grade. The website walks a user through each step of creating a video, from selecting a theme, to uploading short video clips, images, text, and music. After the user adds all of the video elements, Animoto processes and publishes the video to the user's Animoto account. After the video has been published, users can share their videos through a shareable link or export the video to

YouTube or their personal device. Animoto is a useful tool when it is used for a creative project. It is built to offer students entertainment value and has very limited teaching potential. Teachers or students are limited in how they express their ideas or share stories on the platform, taking away from the learning opportunity. Teachers also need to go through lengths to apply for free access to the platform. They are expected to request access to a free account and then set up Gmail addresses for their students to grant them access too. Alternatively, teachers can purchase the professional plan for sixty-five dollars per month which would help them design quality videos as part of lesson content.

Thinglink is a free and user-friendly tool available online and on Android and iOS devices. It is suitable for students between sixth grade and twelfth grade. It allows students and teachers to embed multimedia content on images and videos. The process of embedding multimedia content on existing images and videos is simple. It involves uploading a particular image or video and linking it to other text, images, or videos found on the internet. Links can lead users to a specific website address, audio recordings, or online videos. The educational benefit offered by Thinglink for students and teachers is the addition of the "channels" feature. Channels can be used for individual subjects, class projects, or group activities and they are only accessible to members of that specific group. Therefore when teachers have multiple students from different classes or subjects, they can easily arrange them into separate groups under different channels. The only drawback of using Thinglink is that it takes a while to learn how to maximize the amount of features available on the platform. The free plan provides access to the teacher only while the premium plan allows for up to sixty students to join and for teachers to create, publish, and grade assignments and courses for students.

Storybird is another popular online platform for storytelling. It is suitable for students between kindergarten and twelfth grade. This student-centered social website provides students with the opportunity to be authors and pair their own words with art available on the website. The end result is a unique story in the form of a short story book or poem that teachers can grade or use as a discussion point. The social aspect of this website makes it that much more entertaining for students. After signing into the platform with their teacher-provided credentials, students can browse through other users' stories or create their own. They can also repost some of their favorite stories onto their personal Storybird account feed, as well as "like" or comment on them. The educational benefit of incorporating Storybird into online learning is that the process of creating stories can give rise to various writing tasks or used for peer workshops. With a little bit of creativity on the teacher's part, Storybird can be integrated as part of an exercise or activity in a variety of subjects. With Storybird's school plan, teachers are empowered to create assignments, as well as to review and comment on the stories that the students submit. While the price for the school plan is not available on their website, the individual annual plan is valued at five dollars per month with a once-off annual fee of sixty-dollars rounded up.

Edpuzzle is a web-based tool that lets users create interactive videos and formative assessments. It is suitable for students between third grade and twelfth grade. Users can upload and crop their online videos and add content specific to the predetermined learning objectives. For instance, teachers can upload or create videos on the platform and customize them, adding voice-overs, audio comments, assessment questions, and other relevant resources. The website also offers curriculum content, assigns due dates for assignments, and monitors students' progress. Teachers also have access to students' progress, their personal scores, as well as the records of the length of time it took students to complete assignments.

Teachers can also create and assign quizzes to students and easily export the results to their personal devices when every student has successfully submitted a quiz. One of the unique aspects offered by Edpuzzle is the community of teachers who upload thousands of videos to inspire other teachers on how to create innovative multi-functional videos for educational purposes. The only drawback with this site is that there are hundreds of versions of the same video saved and therefore, it can be rather difficult finding truly innovative content for inspiration. The basic plan is absolutely free and offers teachers many useful features. Those who desire to upgrade their membership can do so by purchasing a Pro Teacher plan for $11.50 per month.

Reading Tools and Apps

RhymeZone is a language reference tool that allows users to search for rhymes as they would search for words in a normal dictionary. It also serves as a search engine for words including similar functions of a thesaurus, spell-checker, and poetry. This tool can be valuable when used to introduce students to the world of poetry or find a suitable rhyme. The search engine is simple to use. All that you are required to do is type a word and the system will bring up rhymes with a similar theme or idea as that word. Thereafter, it is up to you to use your imagination to write your own rendition of the poem or rhyme. You can also use the grammar and vocabulary function to search for the most appropriate words to describe an idea. RhymeZone will also provide you with examples of how to use this word in a phrase or sentence.

Another great reading tool suitable for students between pre-kindergarten and first grade is Kid in Story Book Maker. This storytelling app available on iOS includes a number of story templates that teachers, occupational therapists, or parents can customize to create unique stories. Its green-screen technology has the amazing ability to extract a user's face or body from an image and eliminate the background. This allows for users to drop several images of themselves or others in each scene of the book. Teachers can also choose to create custom books from scratch using their own images and text. It can also be a sweet touch to add a picture of the students throughout the book and bring personality to the characters and storyline. After customizing your story, you can share it with others through the free reader app and allow them to enjoy it in the comfort of their own homes. One of the drawbacks about this app is its hefty price tag at $6.99 per month, as well as the limited number of template designs available for teachers and parents to use.

Raz-Kids is a reading website suitable for students between pre-kindergarten and fifth grade. It offers students access to a virtual library of over four hundred online books. Students have the option of reading their books aloud, listening to the audio version, or simple reading in silence. For assessments, students can record themselves reading the book aloud and upload the recordings on their dashboard. Teachers have access to these recordings and can therefore grade their students' prepared reading accordingly. The platform also offers comprehension quizzes and assessments for every text that includes various multiple-choice questions as well as questions that require in-depth responses regarding the main characters, themes, and ideas revealed in the book. Students also earn stars for making positive progress in their reading and these stars can be used to customize their personal robot avatars or Raz Rockets. While Raz-Kids has a free trial, teachers are required to pay around $115.45 for a full year's access per classroom. This fee does increase when other additional subscriptions are included such as Raz-Plus for personal blended learning. The only drawback about this platform is the lack of higher-level literature in their libraries which may limit students' capacity to engage with more challenging books.

ReadTheory is an online reading and comprehension program suitable for students between kindergarten and twelfth grade. This free platform assesses a student's reading ability and helps students improve their reading comprehension by providing level-appropriate texts for students to read. The platform's algorithm has the ability to sense a student's performance and adapts the difficulty of texts accordingly. As the student reads through each text and answers quiz questions, ReadTheory will present them with passages that test the level of a student's reading. Teachers can simply create a free account and host up to thirty-five student accounts. Students are then added to the online platform by providing their teacher's email address and assigned to their class. Once the registration process has been completed, students will receive a prompt to commence their individual reading pre-test that assesses their reading ability. The results of the pre-test will establish the students' initial reading level. The only drawback about ReadTheory is that sponsored adverts are displayed alongside reading passages which can be very distracting for students who are trying to concentrate on the text or answer quiz questions. Students also aren't able to choose their preferred texts and this may be discouraging for them.

Tools and Apps to Improve Student Behavior, Concentration, and Classroom Management

ClassDojo is a free website that comes packed with many features to document, manage, and improve student behavior and development. It is suitable for students between kindergarten and sixth grade. Teachers can use this tool throughout the class to record and track student behavior, plan classroom activities, customize student portfolios, and collaborate with parents. Teachers also have the option to choose whether they would like to share information privately or publicly. When information is shared publicly, it is displayed to the class through an interactive whiteboard or screen. Students gain or lose points based on their positive or negative behavior. This criteria is usually set by the teacher and communicated to the class. ClassDojo also comes with activities that are designed to improve student development. For instance, topics such as perseverance and how to have a growth mindset are covered in five-minute lessons. Students' behavior can also be tracked at home by parents and communicated to the teacher through the messenger tab. The only drawback with this free website is that students could easily interpret the behavior tracking feature as a system for reward and punishment, particularly when the information is displayed for the whole class to see.

Edmodo is a free learning management system that looks a lot like a social networking website. This platform is suitable for students between third grade and twelfth grade. Teachers can use this platform to manage online instruction. Both students and parents can join a teacher's network by using a class code and upon joining, they can access lesson plans, class deadlines, as well as receive and submit assignments. Once the nitty-gritties have been dealt with, students can interact with their teacher and classmates by participating in group activities and writing posts that include links, images, or other forms of media. Teachers can supervise posts submitted by students on the feed and moderate content or put members on a "read-only" mode. Moreover, teachers can scroll to the Discover page and access useful resources that are student-focused and explore new learning trends, apps, or games. The only drawback about using Edmodo is that since the platform is free, it contains a lot of sponsored adverts on the teacher's interface, making the platform busy and at times, distracting.

Flipgrid is another free website designed to mimic a social networking website. It is suitable for students between third grade and twelfth grade and allows them to customize video responses to questions posed by the teacher. To facilitate these video discussions, a teacher would create a "grid." Each grid becomes similar to a discussion board where teachers can pose questions as "topics" and students can respond with a customized video response that appears in a tiled grid design. Teachers can share grids with the class, groups, or anyone who may be interested in the discussion. Students can record their videos through the Flipgrid website or app or on their mobile devices. Responses can range from fifteen seconds to five minutes in duration. Teachers may also set a limit to the duration of every video response per topic and also grant students permission to record videos in response to their classmates' videos. The only drawback with this platform is that while it offers students a great deal of entertainment value, the educational aspect of the exercise or activity can sometimes be lost in the excitement of the social media-style features of this platform.

MyHomework Student Planner is a valuable tool to help students stay organized, especially when they have very busy schedules. It is ideally suitable for students between seventh grade and twelfth grade. Students can sign in on the mobile app and begin manually adding all of their classes or courses. Once all of the classes have been recorded, students can add other elements to their calendar such as extracurricular activities, upcoming projects, or test dates. Reminders can be set for assignment deadlines or upcoming tests which will help students learn valuable time management skills. The more detailed a student's schedule is, the more organized and structured their days will be. This can improve students' work productivity and effectively hold them accountable for completing and staying up-to-date with their homework demands. The app is completely free to use; however, there are a few drawbacks to expect when using it. Firstly, students may find the process of manually adding their classes to be time-consuming, especially when they have to constantly update their schedule. Secondly, the free version of the app includes a lot of sponsored adverts and teachers should also be careful of a third-party rewards system that pops up on the app.

Assessment, Testing, and Grading Tools

Spiral is a web-based multi-use platform that assists teachers in designing interactive learning experiences. This platform is most suitable for students between third grade and twelfth grade. The basic account is free and offers four types of activities, namely Quickfire, Team Up, Discuss, and Clip. Quickfire allows teachers to create quizzes or questions and send them directly to students. Teachers also have the ability to send back quizzes or questions that were poorly answered to the student and request a resubmission. Team Up helps teachers assign students into groups and have them collaborate on a presentation that gives each student a responsibility. Discuss allows both teachers and students to engage in interactive presentations by discussing ideas, asking questions, and sharing images. Lastly, Clip provides teachers and students with an opportunity to create interactive videos that can lead to an open discussion. Spiral has a free plan for teachers that covers up to five classrooms; however, it also offers the Pro Teacher subscription for thirty-nine dollars per teacher per year. This subscription offers unlimited number of classrooms, free student accounts for at-home use, and progress reports.

Formative is a web-based assessment tool suitable for students between third grade and twelfth grade. Teachers can design or upload assignments that allow students to type, add audio, draw, or enter numbers with a click of a mouse or by using their fingers. The platform is full of ideas for various assessments that teachers can take advantage of. Students can complete assignments by logging into their account; this would also ensure that the teacher keeps track of their progress over time. Alternatively, students can also complete assignments without logging in. Teachers have access to each student's work in real-time available on their dashboard. They also have the convenience of manually or automatically sending students their grades or sharing feedback on assignments through a chat box. With so many great features, designing in-depth assessments is simplified on Formative. However, the only drawback is that assignments are designed for individual assessment and don't offer peer collaboration. Basic features on Formative are free, however, the paid premium subscription valued at $11.25 per month paid yearly, comes with many more features including individual assignments and many more question formats.

Testmoz is a user-friendly web-based assessment tool that teachers can use to create automatically graded tests and quizzes. Teachers can design interactive quizzes in various formats including multiple-choice, true or false, and check box questions. Testmoz also provides teachers with reports that indicate how many students took the test, how long it took for each student to complete it, which questions were answered correctly, and the overall score on their test. Teachers can use this assessment tool alongside any online reading list. Students can open the required reading on one window or tab on their browser, and the Testmoz test or quiz on another. Teachers can also link an article or short story on their Testmoz assessment that would lead to a specific website or the classroom portal. Alternatively, teachers also have the option of allowing students to design their own quizzes which is a fun activity that also consolidates learnings. The free plan allows users to create a basic test that is limited to fifty questions and a hundred results per test. However, for fifty dollars per year users have access to unlimited tests, questions, and results.

Engrade is another web-based grading tool most suitable for students between pre-kindergarten and twelfth grade. It takes the hassle out of class management, collaborating with parents, as well as tracking student performance. Once a teacher has signed up, they can get started on creating a set of standards for their customized gradebook—this feature is known as "Corebook" on the website. After creating a custom Corebook, teachers can set up a virtual class and invite students and parents to register on the website. Engrade allows for continuous communication between teacher and student as well as teacher and parent. Another great feature on the website is the ability for teachers and students to access learning material from third party partners like Khan Academy and BrainPOP that are integrated on the website.

Other impressive tools available for teachers include sending bulk reminders before an assessment, creating a set of review flashcards, creating practice tests, and tracking individual and group grades with ease. The only drawback about using this website is that in order to take advantage of all of these amazing features, consistent collaboration between all stakeholders, including students, teachers, and parents, is required. The platform is free for individual teachers; however, schools and school districts can purchase a subscription for six hundred dollars per year which includes free accounts for up to a hundred students.

Tools and Apps for Better Communication with Parents

Bloomz is a free two-way parent and teacher communication app that offers teachers a convenient way to engage and collaborate with classroom parents. All that parents are required to do is download the app, sign up, and enable their devices to receive notifications and emails from Bloomz. On the teacher's dashboard, they have the ability to control a number of factors regarding the manner in which parents are allowed to communicate. For example, teachers can control whether parents can speak to each other and the kind of information that is shared or accessible for everyone to see on the app. One of the most exciting features available on Bloomz is the parent and teacher conferencing which can be scheduled by the teacher. Moreover, when teachers have a request to make from parents or perhaps they need volunteers for an upcoming project, they can simply send each parent a message on the platform. While there are so many features to use on the website, the only drawback is that teachers can feel overwhelmed very quickly with the constant exchange of information.

Remind is a user-friendly text messaging app that empowers teachers to send targeted or bulk messages to individual students or parents and groups. Remind is extremely safe to use and personal information is never disclosed with any other third party. The app also allows messages to be translated into over seventy languages thus reducing miscommunication as much as possible. Teachers also have the option of choosing how they want to use the app. For instance, teachers may choose a one-way conversation where they treat the app like a virtual bulletin board and share relevant information and updates to parents and students. Alternatively, teachers can choose a two-way conversation where parents and students can respond to posts and engage with the teacher.

With a small fee per transaction, teachers also have an opportunity to collect funds and donations from parents for upcoming events and classroom supplies. Teachers can add users by sharing a link and requesting them to text a unique class code to a five digit number. Students under the age of thirteen years will require email verification from their parents' email account before they can successfully sign up. After a confirmation text has been sent, users will begin receiving notifications and reminders from their teacher through text messages or email. The only drawback with using this app is that without mindful use, messages can become excessive and fail to be productive. Remind is free to use for individual teachers, although a subscription plan for schools and school districts is required.

Seesaw is an online learning system that helps teachers create meaningful multimedia experiences for students that parents can also view and engage with. On Seesaw, teachers can assign students tasks that include work in the form of videos, images, drawings, or text. Once a student has completed the task, they can submit their work on the platform and receive peer-to-peer review and feedback, including encouragement from moms and dads! This collaborative effort in a student's learning experience creates a blog-like atmosphere on the platform that offers students a supportive environment. Some of the safety measures that teachers can enforce includes creating a password to access the blogs and moderating all posts before they are made public for everyone to see. Teachers can also store a digital portfolio of each student's work on Seesaw and share this portfolio with students' parents regularly or when participating in a teacher and parent conference. The only drawback with using this platform is the hefty price tag that it comes with. Individual teachers can enjoy the full benefits of Seesaw and purchase the program for the entire class for $120 per year, while schools and school districts can request a quote.

SimplyCircle, previously known as SchoolCircle, is a user-friendly app and website that provides free communication between parents and teachers. It provides a combination of group email with personal interactions from a private social network of parents. All that teachers are required to do is create a circle and invite your students' parents to join. Teachers are able to send parents group updates, automatic reminders, details of events, and share various media formats. On the teacher's central dashboard, they can track all upcoming events and tasks, plan and manage volunteer signups, and even send targeted messages to individual parents within the larger circle. Another really fantastic feature on SimplyCircle is the ability for teachers to send parents a daily reminder email, daily digest email, and a weekly planner email. This transparent and collaborative effort keeps parents in the loop about upcoming activities, tests, and events, as well as an overview of how their child's school week will look like. Individual teachers can download the app and use it for free, however, their circle is restricted to only twenty members. Paid subscriptions that range from $4.99 to $24.99, allow teachers to add more members to their circle, reaching up to two thousand members and two thousand circle managers.

ParentSquare is an all-encompassing web-based communication portal for teachers to communicate, partner, and engage with parents. It successfully bridges the gap between the school community and home by offering teachers various communication options. For example, teachers can send email notifications, photo, viedo, or file downloads, and post polls for parents to respond to. At an additional cost, teachers can use the Smart Alert feature that sends parents voice-activated messages to communicate urgent information. Teachers can also assess the level of engagement from parents through their teacher's dashboard, as well as to send requests for fundraising initiatives or RSVP invitations. All upcoming events are incorporated into the virtual school calendar and a directory of school staff and families can be uploaded to help parents directly message the specific teacher or parent they wish to speak to. Teachers can also allow parents the ability to post comments on the website or upload class photos onto albums that everyone can view. The only drawback with using this communication tool is that it doesn't include student voices and this may cause parents to assume greater responsibility for the student's learning than they should. To access this website, an initial once-off fee of three hundred dollars per school is required and thereafter there is a four dollar yearly maintenance fee per student and a two hundred dollar yearly maintenance fee per school.

Video Chat Tools and Apps

Cisco, through its Webex productivity tools, is paving the way for online education. many would think of Cisco Webex Teams as being a business tool, however, it is also one of the best platforms to bring students and teachers together through video conferencing. Cisco Webex goes above and beyond offering basic communication features. It encourages digital learning by integrating products such as messaging, calling, and setting up meetings in one stimulating online environment. Teachers can transform the platform into a virtual classroom, facilitating distance learning regardless of where the student may be in the world. On Cisco Webex Teams, students can also collaborate effectively with one another and learn through peer-to-peer engagement and teamwork. Furthermore, the platform facilitates project-based learning where teachers can organize students into small groups and students can ask questions or give feedback on the work without disrupting the whole class. Another interesting feature on Cisco Webex is the virtual whiteboard that is built-into Webex Teams and Webex Meetings. The whiteboard allows teachers to illustrate concepts and ideas by drawing on the board like they would in a normal classroom.

One of the latest developments that is set to launch in the fourth quarter of this year is Cisco Webex Classrooms. This innovative addition to the existing Cisco products is designed to help students and parents connect to teachers and peers. The platform will enable teachers to set up virtual classrooms, determine their virtual office hours, and digitally take notes and record class attendance. Through their personal dashboard, students will have access to their class schedules, video and audio recordings, class assignments, and the ability to engage with their classmates in real-time. Another great feature available on Cisco Webex Classrooms is the security feature that allows teachers to virtually lock their classes, blocking users without an invitation from accessing the class. The security feature also allows teachers to create custom rules such as making users wait in the "lobby" area before they are allowed to enter a virtual class. During the class, teachers can also mute the microphones of the students so that disruptions throughout the duration of the lesson are limited. The platform is also integrated with third party platforms such as Canvas, Blackboard, and Moodle, offering a more enriched learning experience. The price for a

Cisco Webex Teams subscription begins at $13.50 per month per host and spans to $26.95 per month per host depending on the features.

Google Hangouts Meet, or simply Meet, is another great option for teacher and student video conferencing. On Hangouts Meet, schools can maintain a steady flow of communication between all stakeholders involved in a child's educational experience. Distance learning is made fun through this platform because schools have the opportunity to broadcast live lessons for small groups or classes to view in real-time. Teachers can also host one-on-one coaching or mentoring sessions with students or conduct boardroom meetings with their colleagues all in one platform. For asynchronous learning, teachers are able to record instructional videos, lessons, and tutorials for their students to access at their own time or when the students don't have internet connectivity. The benefits for teachers in using Hangouts Meet are remarkably evident. First, setting up a virtual classroom on Hangouts Meet is simple and scheduling regular meetings can be done through sending a calendar invite or sharing a meet link within every Google Classroom.

There is also more than one way of adding students to a meeting. For instance, a teacher may decide to add students using a video link, a special code, or a unique number for more security during conversations. Teachers also have the option of sharing their screen during online lessons and to visually guide students on how to use certain digital tools and softwares during sessions. Hangouts Meet offers teachers access to Google Slides that can be designed and distributed during classes as part of the learning material. Teachers can also set up regular video meetings with parents to discuss student progress and work performance. This would create a collaborative environment that ultimately makes students feel supported in their distance learning.

Hangouts Meet also offers a free digital training tutorial that will train students in using various Google online learning platforms. This will familiarize students with Hangouts Meet and teach them how to start meetings on their own, which will come in handy during group activities. This platform is free for anyone with a Google email address, however on the free plan, meetings are restricted to an hour in length and only a hundred participants can join the team. The G Suite Essentials subscription valued at eight dollars per user per month, allows meetings for up to three hours in length and a hundred and fifty participants can join the team.

Microsoft Teams, which is a feature part of the Microsoft Office package, is another great video conferencing platform for online teaching. Microsoft Teams helps online classes collaborate, manage tasks, plan projects, and engage with one another with great efficiency. The advantage of using Microsoft Teams to host your virtual classroom is that you may be already familiar with some of the other applications that come with Microsoft Office—such as Microsoft Powerpoint, Microsoft Word, and Microsoft Excel—that are user-friendly and offer opportunities for collaboration. Microsoft Teams also gives you access to all of the necessary features for effective video conferencing including, video chatting, hosting audio calls, setting up online meetings, and hosting live events. The platform also accommodates for both synchronous and asynchronous learning, helping students access learning tools and resources whenever they need to.

Microsoft Teams is synonymous with convenience, offering virtual classrooms access to over 250 third party applications that can easily be integrated as part of their account. The service is also available on most technological devices including mobile phones, desktop computers with built-in Windows seven and upward, and on Chrome and Edge. This allows students quick and effortless access to their virtual classroom anytime, and anywhere. Microsoft Teams also allows for teachers to create online professional learning communities where they can support one another and share valuable learning resources, discuss best practices, and learning outcomes. Staff members and leaders can collaborate on classroom curriculum, lesson plans, and administrative work. Microsoft Teams offers a free plan that includes unlimited chat and search, online video conferencing, real-time collaboration with Microsoft Office, and team or personal file storage.

Skype can be a valuable tool to use for video conferencing in the classroom. It goes far beyond the basic video chat standards by offering teachers lesson plans, and so many opportunities to tutor or guide an audience of online learners. Teachers can also use Mystery Skype which is a edutainment feature offered by the platform that brings two virtual classes together to play an online game or solve mysteries together. Many teachers find Skype useful for introducing guest speakers to students over video discussions. Logistically, it may not be possible to have the speaker come to the school and thus through Skype video conferencing, students can still learn from experts. Besides the free one-on-one video call, Skype offers group video conferencing and SMS features on a subscription. Therefore, in order to create a virtual classroom on Skype, teachers or schools will have to pay a premium.

Nonetheless, once you have decided to register an account, signup is fairly simple. After downloading the app on your mobile device or desktop, you can sign in using your existing Skype, Facebook, or Microsoft accounts. Thereafter, you can add contacts to your Skype contact list by searching for a user's Skype name. During video calls, users can send files to one another, share screens, or record the video call. These are all valuable features to have in a virtual classroom. While Skype is one of the earliest video calling apps and the most user-friendly, it is not the most practical for a virtual classroom set up. The app is notorious for having bugs that interfere with the quality of sound and connection between calls. Sometimes calls freeze, get dropped, or lose connection randomly. Due to these technicalities, teachers can't predict the flow of their lessons when hosting sessions on Skype, making it unreliable and disruptive. Nonetheless, it may be a great platform to use when practicing how to conduct an online teaching lesson.

One of the latest video-conferencing tools to enter the market is Zoom. The platform gained significant popularity during the wake of the global Coronavirus pandemic where business units were scurrying to find the best video-conferencing tool to host daily meetings and planning sessions. Zoom has also become one of the go-to platforms for online learning where coaches, therapists, and teachers continue to host their classes, seminars, and sessions with minimal effort required. One of the notable benefits of using Zoom for distance learning is that it is simple to set up, it can accommodate up to a hundred participants in one call, and it is a low-cost option. The free version of Zoom offers teachers the opportunity to have individual and group meetings, allow students to signal when they have a question without using words, host brainstorming sessions on a virtual whiteboard, allow students to collaborate on projects, and so much more! One of the most recent developments on the platform was the removal of the forty-minute time restriction on meetings hosted on the free account version. This means that teachers can host sessions for an unlimited duration.

The paid subscription version of Zoom offers even more convenience for individual teachers, as well as schools and school districts. For instance, on a paid subscription, teachers or schools can record meetings, access the admin dashboard for more control over meetings, establish a signal sign on, and so much more. Zoom is accessible on any technological device with internet connectivity, a camera, and audio capacity; this means that you can download your Zoom app on any smartphone, desktop computer, laptop, or tablet. Generally, it is not necessary for students to register an account if the meeting is organized and scheduled by the teacher; however, they must have the app installed on their technological device in order to access the meeting through a shared link or by typing in a special meeting password. Students under the age of sixteen are not permitted, by Zoom policy, to register an account on their own. Therefore, teachers would need to consult parents and the school district to establish the best process to follow for these students to follow. As mentioned above, Zoom is free to use for individual teachers who want to set up a quick and efficient virtual classroom, giving them plenty of features to make the process as enriching as possible. Subscription plans offer many more features such as social media streaming, recording transcripts, and unlimited cloud storage. These plans start from $149.90 and go up to $199.90 per year per license.

Chapter Four:

Maintaining Student

Engagement

There is a plethora of research studies that have been done investigating student engagement in the classroom. This is a topic that never gets old in teacher circles because student engagement is what every teacher (whether teaching from a desktop computer or in a classroom) desires. Teachers want to see and feel that their students are engaged so that they can assess the quality of the work being taught and whether the students are learning anything valuable. When students are disengaged for example, it may signify to the teacher that the work is not interesting enough or that it doesn't effectively meet the learning outcomes. Conversely, when students are engaged during classes, it may signify to the teacher that the work is stimulating and provides enough motivation for students to learn and progress through the module or unit. Achieving a high level of student engagement in the traditional classroom is hard enough. With the global transition to distance learning, teachers are finding it even more challenging to keep students engaged during online learning.

Online learning presents teachers with new challenges of trying to discipline, manage, and engage with students over a computer screen. Online teachers are constantly seeking for new ways to connect with their students and make the virtual classroom feel intimate and safe. They want to engage with their students through activities and assessments so that their class feels supported and motivated to continue learning. One of the greatest challenges presented with online learning is the social barrier that it creates. The teacher and student are separated and sometimes don't have the opportunity to interact in real-time. This social barrier causes some students to feel frustrated or isolated in their learning experience. In my many years of online teaching, I have found that building a community in your online teaching helps both the teacher and student feel connected with one another, even when the two are living in separate locations or timezones. The virtual community includes an instructor and a network of students that are partaking in the class, module, or course. Sometimes this community may also include student teachers, mentors, and teaching assistants who are available to answer student questions and guide them when the teacher is unavailable.

Building a virtual community is simple, and I would encourage you to try the following steps on your next online lesson! Firstly, you will need to formally introduce yourself to each student before your online lesson begins. Send them an email or message through your online portal's chat service and tell them a little more about you and the value that they will receive by taking your lesson. You can also add instructions on how to navigate through the lesson and prepare them for an assessment that will be required for them to take at the end. This introduction may be written; however, filming a short video clip would add a personal touch. Secondly, you will need to create an icebreaker or introductory activity that allows your students to connect with each other and get excited about going on this learning journey. You can do this by creating a Blackboard discussion forum where you can ask students to introduce and mention something interesting about themselves. Another great idea is to ask students to upload an image of something that they find truly inspirational and ask them to explain why they chose that image.

Lastly, throughout the module or learning unit, you will need to provide countless opportunities for student interaction. When students feel supported by their peers, they can easily cope with the demands or expectations that come with some assignments and activities. Regularly post discussions, ask group questions, and encourage group activities. It is also important to switch up the ways in which you request students to interact with one another. For instance, on one occasion you may ask them to give a written response on a thread, and on another occasion you may ask them to send a video or audio recording of their response. Switching up the style and format of the interactions will encourage students to be creative in how they develop their responses, while also keeping them entertained.

Despite the social barrier created with online learning, there is also an administrative barrier presented which can cause frustration and hopelessness in students. The reason why we emphasize the importance of planning lessons well in advance is because poor administration during an online lesson, module, or course can cause students to disengage or simply drop out of your class. Imagine how frustrating it must be to not have sufficient instructional information about how to complete the lesson or how to submit assignments. Students thrive when their online classes are organized, well-structured, and predictable. They may also want to know their progress during the class and gain valuable feedback from their teacher. Having clear and open lines of communication, as well as a smooth system of running the class will set your students up for success and keep them engaged throughout.

Some of the ways that you can overcome the administrative barriers is to provide your contact information and office hours so that students know when and how to reach you when they have questions. If you are not always available online, provide alternative ways that students can leave messages for you or assistant teachers. Platforms like Google Hangouts Meet allow teachers to share their calendars with students and for them to book slots for one-on-one meetings during open office hours. Another tip for removing administrative barriers is to break down instructions in the most clear manner possible. Once students have read instructions for an activity, they should never be left with questions on what they are expected to do. Keep your directions concise while also explaining them in multiple channels such as email or classroom portal. Also ensure that your directions and instructions are explained in multiple formats. For example, if you have given your instructions on a video, make sure that below the video or on the page, you have the same directions or instructions written. Lastly, ensure that you respond to your students' questions and comments in a timely fashion. Constantly provide students with reassurance and feedback on their performance so that they remain motivated to complete the course.

Why Keeping Students Engaged Is So Difficult

One of the main priorities for teachers in a classroom setting is to engage the disengaged students. There are a number of reasons why students disengage from learning material but the online experience makes it even more challenging. When some other distraction other than their online lesson is only one click away, how do teachers maintain student engagement online? Firstly, it may be important to describe a disengaged student's behavior so that online teachers know the early signs to look out for during online lessons. While it is normal for students to be quiet in class, get bored over learning material, or have moments of losing their attention, a disengaged student finds no value in the work, nor do they see the purpose of the learning material. This makes them slow to complete tasks, often delaying or postponing their work until the last minute or failing to complete tasks on time. Disengaged students take a passive approach to learning. They require the teacher to do more of the leg work while they invest minimal effort and are quite satisfied with average results.

Disengaged students also find group work or exercises challenging because most of the time these exercises require their active participation. In groups, these students need more encouragement to share their views and ideas with their peers. Disengaged students are also resistant to new learning experiences that require them to go out of their comfort zone. For instance, a spot quiz or random assessment may cause them to withdraw and at times, become defensive. Teachers can also identify disengagement students by their apathetic attitude toward school work and tasks. For instance, a disengaged student would remark, "This exercise is boring," or "Why do we have to do this?" Most of the time, disengaged students are not clear on the expectations for learning. They don't see the importance of the content or how it can enrich their lives. This causes them to show a lack of ambition or self-determination in completing their assigned work or attaining goals that other students are aiming for.

Having students in attendance but disengaged from the class or the work can be a stressful experience for teachers. After having checked every box that you needed as an educator and provided the most stimulating class environment, there will still be students who are not present at all. However, it is important to remember that besides having learning difficulties, students may be disengaged due to personal challenges experienced at home or within their communities which cause a lot of fear and anxiety in the learner's mind, causing them to lose focus or interest in school work. This is especially true in this Covid-19 era we are living in and the amount of disruptions that have been caused in students' personal lives. Below are three personal reasons that cause students to disengage during class that have nothing to do with the teacher or course itself.

One reason that may be causing students to disengage in online classes is due to a change in their life circumstances. There are many environmental factors that may be causing disharmony in your students' personal lives. These include the global Coronavirus pandemic, the economic recession, parents losing their jobs, crime in their communities, family dysfunction, and so forth. There is a big possibility that your students' lives may have changed significantly since the time when schools had to shut down. They may have had to move to a different home, their parents may have gotten a divorce, or their livelihood may have drastically been compromised. It is not a secret that many households are struggling to meet financial obligations, gain access to food, bury loved ones, and take care of sick relatives. In terms of doing school work, students may not have access to the internet in their homes or communities or a decent workspace to use for learning. Other students may be in a different time zone and thus cannot meet at a specific time and others may find it difficult to focus on lessons with all of the background noise and distractions in their households.

In a physical classroom, teachers have the opportunity to check-in on their students and find out how they are doing. They are also able to pick up on changes in behavior and intervene when a student looks worn out or stressed. Teaching online makes it difficult for teachers to sense what the student may be experiencing, especially because students may hide their true feelings once the webcam has been switched on. It may also be impossible for the student to openly share their anxieties and fears with their teacher because of a lack of privacy at home. The second reason why students may be disengaged is due to dealing with stress and trauma in their personal lives. It is a known fact that stress and trauma can disturb cognitive processing, discourage students from participating or taking pride in their work, and cause them to have emotional outbursts. Now more than ever, students are battling to cope with the growing pressures experienced from their environment and this causes a lot of emotional challenges. Without the necessary coping strategies being taught or put in place, students project their fears and anxieties during classes and adopt unhealthy methods of dealing with stress.

Another reason why students may find it difficult to engage in online classes is due to the lack of academic and emotional support at home. Many students enjoy going to school because they know that there is a level of order and structure established there which makes learning more convenient. Distance learning has forced students and parents to adopt the same level of order and structure instilled at school at home. This has been a challenge for many households because both students and parents were not prepared for the adjustment in learning style that would be required of them. Students have also had to be more independent and responsible for their school work, especially in homes where the parents are not available for academic support. The pressure of self-teaching or completing assignments alone can cause students to feel discouraged and frustrated by the school demands.

Strategies to Maximize Student Engagement During Online Learning

It is understandable for students to feel like virtual school is boring or lacking the elements of fun that traditional school brought. Without the exhilarating social interactions, the consistent and predictable schooling environment, and the face-to-face guidance from teachers, many of the motivational drivers for learning had been taken away. Furthermore, the slow-start to setting up virtual classrooms, organizing access to computers or internet at home, and the partnership with parents has made many students question the appropriateness or sustainability of online teaching. Teachers play a significant role in silencing students' fears and anxieties when it comes to online learning. While some of the challenges that students face are personal in nature and out of the teacher's control, teachers can ensure that the learning experience available to students accommodates their academic needs and offers plenty of opportunities to interact with other learners and share common experiences.

Doing this successfully requires teachers to design online curriculums that reduce instructional flaws of accountability and standardized testing and do away with the traditional carrots and sticks method of enforcing discipline and interaction in virtual classrooms. Demoralizing demands and highly-weighted assessments will not encourage students to absorb knowledge and desire to learn more. There are other approaches that online teachers can take to motivate their students to fall in love with learning experience and keep them engaged throughout the various challenges that they will be faced with during distance learning. The two approaches to motivating students and maximizing their engagement are to instill a learning mindset in each student and sharpen the learning context. Instilling a learning mindset involves transforming the beliefs that students hold about themselves and their performance at school. It is about showing students their true potential and ability to succeed and fully grasp the nature of their work. Sharpening the learning context involves making students understand the value in the learning material and clearly laying out learning outcomes, and goals that they can achieve through the learning material offered.

Online teachers can adopt and train their students to operate in three learning mindsets which will make them highly responsive to tasks and assignments given during class and help them build enough confidence in themselves to work independently. The first learning mindset that teachers need to adopt is to create a sense of belonging among students. Teachers need to make students feel heard and that their opinions are valid during class discussions. This can be done by designing class material that accommodates various students' personal interests and includes topics and activities that students identify with. This would make students feel that it is safe for them to come out of their shell and share their authentic nature with the class on a daily basis. Teachers also need to be careful not to include material that would threaten or offend any of their students' identity, culture, religion, race, or sexual orientation. It is important for every child to feel as though they are just as valuable and respected by the teacher and their peers as the next child.

Another way to create a sense of belonging is to reduce barriers to connecting online. Teachers need to regularly communicate that they are available to students outside of class time. Sharing office hours, contact details, and opening time slots for one-on-one discussions will make your students feel supported even after the class is over. You can manage student expectations by telling them when you will be available to respond to their questions and the days when you will not be available. It may also be important to remind students that they can come to you with any kind of questions, even if it is not related to class or school work. Make it known on various communication channels that you welcome student interaction and value what they have to share with you. This can make students comfortable to approach you with other emotional challenges that they are facing in their lives.

Lastly, a sense of belonging is created through socializing. Therefore, it is important for you to dedicate as much time to social interaction as you do to academic work. Be flexible in how you divide your time between purely teaching and allowing your students to enjoy back and forth discussions with each other. For example, offering students monitored hangout time before and after lessons could be a great incentive to make them concentrate during teaching hours. During the lesson, you can also incorporate a five-minute "mental-stretch" break where students can go and grab a glass of water and take a moment to gather themselves. You can also create weekly asynchronous social gatherings where your students meet to discuss their upcoming assessments, ask each other questions, and share learning experiences.

The second learning mindset that teachers need to adopt and teach their students is to associate school work to purpose. It is extremely important for students to understand the 'why' factor to everything that they are doing. This helps students determine how much effort they need to put into the task or assignment. Teachers tend to underestimate the importance of explaining the value behind their content because they assume it is obvious or doesn't require justification. However, when students don't know why they are doing a task, it may cause them to disconnect from the work. Regularly stress the importance of themes and topics covered in class and give practical examples of how students can apply this knowledge in their ordinary lives. It may also be reassuring to have students complete practical activities and exercises that demonstrate the knowledge learned during lessons.

Another way to associate school work to purpose is to make a distinct connection between the work covered during classes and real-life circumstances and scenarios. Research has shown that students are more motivated to complete tasks during class when a clear link was drawn between what they were learning and their personal interests or the events taking place in the world (Kelleher & Hulleman, 2020). To make this association, teachers will need to stay up-to-date with current affairs or listen attentively to the discussions that students have in order to create meaningful content that addresses some of their interests, hobbies, and the trends that they follow.

The final learning mindset that you need to adopt and teach to your students is the growth mindset. Teachers need to make sure that their students understand that failure is natural and can be overcome with determination and hard work. Everyone makes mistakes or fails at something at least several times in their life. It is normal to have high expectations and for those expectations not to be met. In most cases, with failure will come disappointment and even this feeling is natural. Teachers need to ensure that students understand that their work is not a reflection of who they are. Studying anything in life is hard, however over time, it gets easier. It may help to teach students about neuroplasticity and how our brains are re-wired to think differently when we adopt new learning habits and put consistent effort in practicing and studying school work. Teachers can also dedicate a lesson every week for practicing study skills and teaching students studying strategies. These lessons should be dedicated to exposing students to various methods and options available to make their learning experience easier and more empowering. These lessons will also help those students who don't have any academic support at home learn strategies on how to work efficiently without parental supervision.

Tips on Creating Engaging Content During Online Learning

Capturing student engagement requires various approaches at various levels. Once you have adopted the three learning mindsets in your class, it is your responsibility to continuously reinforce them in every element of your online teaching. However, you will also need to supplement those mind tools with effective learning tools that can improve upon the learning context in your virtual classroom. Creating a learning context involves creating an environment where what you are teaching is understood by your students without any misunderstandings. The learning context impacts on how well your students are able to grasp, process, and apply the learning material. Therefore, to create the most appropriate learning context for your virtual classroom, you will need to pay attention to the learning style and structure that you implement. You should use a style and structure that inspires students to engage with the learning material instead of passively receiving it.

For instance, students are likely to be more engaged in your online classes when they have been sufficiently prepared before the class begins. You can prepare your students in advance by offering them downloadable lesson plans, classroom rules and expectations, learning outcomes for the lesson or course, as well as any copies of rubrics for grading assessments. It may also be useful to make discussion questions available beforehand in order for students to have time to prepare and plan their responses. Alternatively, you can ask students to prepare discussion questions or topics well in advance so that when the time comes, you have a high rate of engagement from most students. Another suggestion is to make most of the beginning portion of your lesson. Many students may be feeling anxious at the beginning of a new course or module because of their perceived feelings about the course or module. Use the introductory lesson to paint an exciting picture about what students can anticipate in the upcoming weeks. Make introductions light-hearted and full of entertainment value in order to change students' perceptions on the course.

You can also get students engaged with the content by spacing it out so that it doesn't follow one style from beginning to end. For example, instead of presenting information in the form of a lecture throughout the lesson, you can divide the content by first presenting the information and following it by an activity or an online learning game to make the lesson more diversified and interesting. Another tip is to get students excited about taking action and actively breaking down the content during lessons or afterward. Encourage students to answer questions or give feedback in a live video session after class or open the discussion board for students to leave remarks about the images, videos, and information they were exposed to during class.

For a more in-depth sharing experience, you can give students a homework assignment of writing a short essay or opinion piece regarding the film, interview, or conversations that they were exposed to in class and allow them to share this piece with the class the following day. During class, you can encourage students to take action by forming mini discussion groups and assigning them a topic or theme to analyze and form an opinion on. You can also consider other online tools such as starting a private Facebook group, starting a classroom YouTube account with the help of students, or creating a classroom blog where you and the students can share information on relevant classroom topics.

Chapter Five:

Facilitating Discussions and Participation

When learning online, many students may feel discouraged from actively participating in the lesson. One of the main reasons, as mentioned in the previous chapter is due to not being engaged in the class or interested in the class work. However, there are several other reasons why students may be hesitant or resistant to participate in class discussions. The first reason is simple: they aren't clear on the lesson or course expectations. They are not sure how to upload work, where to post, or what posts should include. This reason is more common than teachers might think. Out of fear of looking silly or seeming disengaged, students will delay taking any action until more information is provided by the teacher. Even if the necessary instructions were given at the beginning of the module or learning unit, it is natural for students to forget what they saw or read given the amount of information that has been uploaded since then. One way that teachers can prevent this from happening is to dedicate a page or section on the classroom portal to post frequently asked questions, guidelines on how to access online educational tools, how to submit work, and common class etiquette.

Teachers can also include practical examples of how they expect students to respond to discussions or questions. For instance, a teacher may post an example of a typical opinion-based post and another example of a post that could be used for assessment. Another common reason why students fail to participate during virtual classes is because they feel as though they have nothing to contribute or share. This may be due to shyness or certain insecurities with speaking on video conference calls. Many students who are new to online learning may experience this as they try to navigate the new digital learning environment and how to use all of the available tools. Furthermore, students who are unfamiliar with the topic may find it intimidating to share their views, especially when they notice other children having more concrete ideas and opinions. Teachers can accommodate shy students by making sure that they feel safe to participate. Taking the time to create fun introductions in the beginning may help to make students more relaxed and open during the course of the lesson.

Sometimes, students don't participate during online classes because they are either experiencing technical difficulties or they are unfamiliar with the platform or online tools. We tend to assume that every child is born having coding skills but this is not true. Many students struggle with technology, especially when they have had very little exposure to it. Other times, the platform that the teachers use to host their classes are not compatible with the technological device or website browser that the student is using. This may cause glitches or error messages to pop up, ultimately preventing students from accessing the class. There are also those students who don't understand how a threaded conversation works, aren't aware of the subscription features of the platform, or how to join meetings using a link and a password. In these cases, clearly communicated instructions with the assistance of a video tutorial or screen grabs will help your students access the correct platforms and use all of the tools and features available to them. When students are having technical difficulties, it is important to assist them as soon as you can, preferably within twenty-four hours so that they do not miss out on too much work.

Lastly, students may be discouraged from participating in class discussions due to being intimidated or offended by their classmates' comments to previous posts. Online texting can easily be misinterpreted because the receiver of the text doesn't have a clear understanding of the sender's intentions, nor can they rely on non-verbal cues like facial expressions to clarify the message. Moreover, cultural differences among students can also cause messages to be misinterpreted. Depending on the household, community, or culture that a student has been exposed to, they may have a different standard of acceptable and unacceptable communication. Students that are offended will typically shut down and withdraw from participating in group discussions or opinion-related conversations. Many times, the teacher is not aware that this offense has taken place because the student won't express their discomfort around certain topics or among certain classmates. One way that teachers can prevent such offenses from taking place is to create standards and guidelines for interactions between students online. Teachers should also monitor online group discussions and moderate posts that students post on all educational platforms. Students who post troublesome posts or try to dominate group discussions should be addressed on a one-on-one video call and corrected immediately.

Promoting Participation in Online Classes

Teachers find it challenging to get students to participate in a traditional classroom setting and this challenge is deepened when the classroom takes place through a computer screen. Before online teaching, you could easily identify those students who were trying to go unnoticed in the background or needed extra encouragement in order to speak. On a video conference call, teachers cannot rely on their intuitive sixth sense to pick on how students are feeling toward the topic or the conversation at hand. It can be especially frustrating for teachers when they spend several minutes explaining a concept and after pausing for a moment, feel as though they are the only person on the conference call. Silence from students is never a good indication that learning is taking place and teachers may become demoralized when they realize that they are teaching to a confused or disinterested audience. Nonetheless, teachers can rescue their virtual class from completely going to ruins by encouraging voluntary participation.

Voluntary participation is when students willingly engage with the content or the teacher because of the many opportunities that the teacher has created for students to actively participate. When teachers plan a lesson, their general objectives are to share knowledge, encourage students to make decisions and solve problems, and to deepen students' understanding about life. To meet all of these objectives, teachers need active students who can engage with the learning material and actually do the work. Teachers can apply five tested rules that will encourage voluntary participation during online classes and make each lesson a valuable learning resource. The sixty-second rule states that within the first sixty-seconds of presenting your lesson, provide context to the problem by sharing a story, an experience, or eyebrow-raising statistics to allow students to emotionally invest in the content. The first sixty-seconds become a selling pitch where you allow students to understand the problem or the opportunity before you give them arguments or strategies to solve it.

The responsibility rule states that online lessons where both teacher and student have the same shared responsibility to contribute experience a higher rate of engagement. It is human nature that when anyone enters a social setting, they will immediately assume the most fitting role. For example, when you go to a restaurant for a meal, you automatically assume the role of one being served and allow the waiter to be the server. Similarly, in virtual classrooms, students assume that their role is to passively listen and observe the teacher speak while they sit quietly and absorb the knowledge. To reverse this subconscious decision, teachers need to create a culture of shared responsibility early on in the lesson. Instead of telling students that you expect them to share their views and ask questions, you can create a number of opportunities during your lesson for students to take responsibility.

The "Nowhere to Hide" rule states that students need to be given a certain amount of responsibility in the form of tasks in order for them to willingly participate. Typically, when the responsibility is diffused in a classroom, students don't feel the need to participate. For example, when you pose a question for anyone in the classroom to answer, you will have to wait a few minutes before anyone voluntarily raises their hand. However, if you hand-picked students and gave them the responsibility to prepare answers to certain questions, they will feel more obliged to engage with the content. The trick here is to not give students anywhere to hide. Define a problem that students can solve quickly, assign them into small groups and allow them to discuss solutions with one another. If you are using a teaching platform that offers breakout rooms, this would be a great chance to use them. Remember that the more detailed and defined the task is, the easier it will be for students to participate and have something meaningful to share.

The Minimum Viable Powerpoint rule or MVP rule, states that the less information a powerpoint presentation has, the easier it is for students to engage with it. There is nothing that leads to disengagement faster than a presentation with slides full of chunky information and endless bullet points. Even the most enthusiastic students will become exhausted from the lack of mind stimulation or variety in how information is delivered. Teachers need to create visual presentations with the least amount of data possible. This means that only the most crucial points, concepts, or ideas should be displayed on each slide. This will also force teachers to engage with the students more and encourage them to fill in the gaps or unpack concepts in more depth. Having too many slides also takes away creativity in how information is presented. When a teacher has too many slides, they may feel pressured to go through each one. I have found that students learn through data and stories. It is important to break away from the data every now and again to tell a story or share an experience. This brings life to the content and allows students to see the value in what they are learning.

The fifth rule is the five-minute rule. This rule states that teachers should never go longer than five-minutes before giving students another problem to solve. The biggest challenge with virtual classrooms is that students are exposed to so many distractions within their environment and online. Thus, online teachers need to regularly check-in with students to ensure that they are still tuned into the class. There needs to be a continuous expectation for students to interact with the teacher and the content, otherwise students will withdraw back to their comfortable passive role. In a thirty-minute class for example, a teacher would need to incorporate six brief and meaningful engagement opportunities. On one occasion, the teacher can organize students in groups for a quick discussion among themselves and on another one, the teacher can take a quick poll or allow the students to complete a short quiz.

These rules will help teachers create a culture of voluntary participation in online classes and with regular practice, students won't need as much encouragement to interact with the teacher, ask questions, or engage with the content. However, there are also innovative strategies that teachers can adopt for specifically synchronous and asynchronous learning. As we have discussed in a previous chapter, synchronous learning refers to online teaching that happens in real-time where the teacher and the students are engaging with the learning material at the same time. There are a number of strategies that will help teachers get students to participate during synchronous learning. The first strategy is for the teacher to facilitate a spider-web discussion. Allow students to prepare their opinion on a subject or discussion point. In the first ten-minutes of your class the following day, get students to start the meeting by sharing their perspectives one at a time. After each student speaks, ensure that the following speaker either adds onto the point made by the previous speaker or shares a completely new point that can lead the discussion elsewhere. Eventually, a web of ideas and opinions will form and as the teacher, you are able to assess which students spoke and which ones didn't contribute. You can then personally ask the quiet students specific questions to elicit specific responses. Ultimately, at the end of the ten-minutes all students should have contributed their views to some extent.

Another strategy for synchronous learning is to use the online chat feature during video conferencing to check whether students understand the information being taught. After a few minutes of teaching, pause for a brief moment and ask students to type "Yes" if they understand the concepts or "No" if they are confused or completely lost. Another way to gage students' level of participation is to ask them to send emojis describing how they are feeling toward the content being taught. Some may enter an excited emoji while others may enter an indifferent or sad emoji. Based on what students are feeling, you can go over concepts again or teach it in a different manner, perhaps incorporating a game or practical exercise. Teachers can also pose true or false questions to the class and request that students share their responses in the chat box. There are also some teaching platforms, such as Zoom, which offer a raising hand feature that signals when students have a question to ask the teacher. Encouraging students to use this feature can also be a great way to check for understanding.

There are also a number of strategies to encourage participation during asynchronous learning. Asynchronous learning refers to online teaching that does not occur in real-time. Usually, the teacher and students will not go over the learning material at the same time or in the same place. This gives students the flexibility to complete modules and class exercises at their own pace in their own time. While synchronous learning offers both teachers and students a similar interaction to a traditional classroom, asynchronous learning can in some cases increase the level of participation from students because there are no time-constraints to when they can answer questions and share their responses. Students who are shy to share in groups may also feel more comfortable sharing their opinions outside of the boundaries of a full class. An effective strategy for encouraging participation during asynchronous learning is to create an online forum or facilitate ongoing classroom discussions where students can regularly enjoy a back and forth dialogue with the teacher and their peers. Teachers can stimulate dialogue by responding to each student post with a clarifying or probing question that requires students to provide more context or information.

Teachers can also encourage students to respond to at least two other students' feedback or comments to create a more enriching discussion. Another way to facilitate discussions is to encourage students to share images to show what they have learned from the learning material. Sharing images will allow students to reflect on the significance of the content they are learning and draw connections between the images and the written information. An alternative to using images can be using videos or voice recordings of students that also provide an opportunity for students to engage with one another and actively participate during classes. Another great strategy to promote participation in asynchronous classes is to create an online brainstorming session which continues for a couple of days. This brainstorming session may be valuable at the beginning of a new learning unit or module to build anticipation around the content. You can create a shared online document with a series of questions or prompts. Thereafter, encourage students to leave their thoughts under each question within a specified time frame. These answers would then become the main focus of the discussion about the particular theme, idea, or concept.

Encouraging Participation by Learning Your Students' Personality Types

It is important for teachers to present lessons in a way that encourages each student to engage with the content. This is not an easy feat to undertake because every student has their own learning style which may or may not compliment the teacher's style of delivery. Many times, students fail to participate in classes because they are not motivated to learn. Identifying your students personality type may help you as the educator presents your lessons in a way that encourages participation. Familiarizing yourself with the various personality types of your students, and fine-tuning your content delivery accordingly, is just as important online as it is in traditional classrooms. Some of the common personality tests available for educational purposes are the Myers-Briggs, Big Five, True Colors, and the Enneagram test. However, the most popular seems to be the Myers-Brigg Type Indicator. As a teacher of juniors, it may be difficult to administer a Myers-Brigg Type Indicator with your young student but there are a few basic traits that you can look out for in your virtual classroom.

The Myers-Brigg personality test focuses on four significant areas in a student's life namely; their orientation to life, perception, decision-making abilities, and their attitude toward their environment. When looking at the first part of the test which focuses on a student's orientation to life, there is one main question that is asked: is the student an extrovert or introvert? The good news is that this kind of information is easily observed within the first few minutes of a new synchronous course or lesson. Typically, students who are enthusiastic about making introductions with the teacher or quick to provide personal information about themselves are extroverted. Conversely, students who are more timid to answer questions or who need more encouragement to share their views are introverted. Learning how to effectively teach students who are both extroverts and introverts requires teachers to step into the student's shoes. Imagine how it would feel like to have a class over a computer screen for the first time. Imagine how it would feel to build a relationship with a teacher through video calls. This experience is exhilarating for some and frightening for others.

An introverted student may start opening up after the teacher has shown that they are friendly and approachable. Using a universal smile, speaking slowly, and being conscious of one's tone of voice can make introverted students feel more comfortable engaging with the teacher. On the other hand, extroverted students won't need as much encouragement to participate, however, they will need rules established that govern communication etiquette and when it is not appropriate to share an opinion or ask questions during class. The second part of the Myers-Brigg personality test looks at students' perception of their environment. By assessing a student's perception, the test is attempting to figure out whether the student is intuitive or sensing. Intuitive students perceive the lesson in a broader and abstract way and those who are sensing perceive the lesson in a more concrete or factual way. Teachers can accommodate intuitive students by giving a general overview of the lesson at the beginning of the session and sharing the general purpose or value behind the lesson.

Sensing students will absorb the content better when they are given practical examples of how to apply the knowledge in their lives. Instead of explaining the concept in philosophical terms, sensing students prefer seeing the concept in action and applied in a real way. Therefore, to accommodate both intuitive and sensing students, a teacher can give a brief introduction on the lesson followed by clearly defined objectives and learning outcomes that will be covered. The fourth part of the Myers-Brigg personality test looks at a student's decision-making ability. Students form decisions in multiple ways. For instance, one student may form a decision based on their feelings, and another may come to a decision after a rigorous thought process. Feeling students have an unconventional way of coming to conclusions which doesn't follow a step-by-step process. You can support these students in making decisions by encouraging them to listen to their gut feeling after having learned a concept. Thinking students may take a longer time sharing their subjective views on a subject matter because they don't process information based on feelings.

Thinking students need to follow processes in order to come to a conclusion or answer a question asked by the teacher. Therefore, you can encourage thinking students to make decisions by walking them through the various steps of resolving the problem at hand. For instance, in a math lesson, a thinking student would need to go through each step carefully to come to a reasonable conclusion while a feeling student may base their mathematical problem-solving on emotional inclinations. Teachers need to be mindful that sometimes feeling students are able to arrive at conclusions without being able to explain or show evidence of how they came to it. The fourth part of the Myers-Brigg personality test looks at a student's attitude toward the world around them. Every person leans toward either a judgemental or perception-based attitude toward their environment. This is similar to whether a student is intuitive or sensing. In the learning environment or within a virtual classroom, students tend to carry a logical or emotional attitude to solving problems or meeting class expectations. Students who are more judgemental and logical will desire a more structured learning environment whereas those who rely on their perceptions and emotions to navigate through the learning environment will desire a less rigid approach.

Teachers can achieve a high rate of engagement in their virtual classrooms by remembering one valuable lesson: every student is different and therefore has different needs. A teacher may design the best lesson plan but find that only half of the students engaged with the content. Students have varying learning styles and therefore there isn't a clear-cut formula or secret to creating lessons that incorporate every student's method of learning. It is simply a matter of trial-and-error, practicing multiple approaches and finding those that incorporate the needs of the majority of the students. It also means that teachers cannot become too comfortable teaching courses or lessons in one manner. There are so many creative ways of teaching learning material that could be more engaging for students. Furthermore, when teachers step out of their comfort zones, they can design lessons from the perspective of their students and therefore provide a more relatable and fun lesson.

How to Encourage Parents to Participate in Their Children's Online Learning Experience

Parent and family participation has always played a major role in the success of a student's educational career. However, now that many students are learning from home due to school closures, the support of parents in a student's learning experience has taken on a new meaning. Parents have been required to take on a much greater responsibility in supervising their children's school work and offering assistance when students have to perform tasks. This new responsibility thrusted on parents and families can be overwhelming and thus, online teachers must find ways of offering support and guidance to families when helping their children succeed with online learning. The first step that teachers can take in supporting families is to clearly articulate the challenges and opportunities that online learning will bring. Teachers should remind parents that online learning follows different processes and uses different systems than traditional learning. Parents should be aware upfront of the differences between the two and the expectations that come with their child's online learning.

Teachers should also discuss the opportunities that online learning offers to the child's overall learning experience. Educational lessons can be integrated into real-life activities and experiences with mom, dad, or older siblings. For instance, when families play board games together it can promote a range of academic and social skills. Moreover, when parents read a book with their child and ask them questions throughout, it can help children formulate strong ideas and opinions about a variety of themes and concepts. When families are involved in their children's at-home learning experience, they can turn every day home activities into educational opportunities and encourage learning to take place even after the online lesson has happened. Another suggestion for teachers is to encourage parents to support their children's at-home learning by creating experiences for the child instead of lecturing them on school work. Parents should place emphasis on the quality of time spent with their children and turning those intimate encounters into teachable moments. For example, baking chocolate-chip cookies with a child can be a great way to teach them about fractions.

I have also found through my years of online teaching that parents are more willing to participate in a student's learning experience when they have been given sufficient tools and clear expectations on how they can support the student in each activity. Teachers need to provide parents with an adequate amount of resources, access to portals or platforms, and a detail of the curriculum or lesson plans so that they are equipped with enough knowledge to help their children learn better. For example, when teachers require elementary students to complete an activity, they can include an instructional sheet for parents who will be working with students on the activity. Briefly explain what the activity is about and what students will take away from it. Thereafter, give parents tips on how to help their children complete the activity and a picture of the activity once it is complete. It may be useful to also provide a checklist to ensure that parents have completed all of the steps or processes required in the exercise.

Lastly, teachers need to set clear communication expectations with parents. It is important for parents and families to know when and how they can contact you as the educator. The more structure you establish in the communication between you and the student's family, the easier it will be to address concerns, update parents on new learning material, and share your feedback on the child's performance in class. Establishing clear communication expectations will also prevent you from becoming overwhelmed by messages from parents. You can communicate your availability to parents through email or on parent and teacher platforms. Set office hours and expected time for responding to messages. For example, you can say that messages received after four p.m will be answered the following day. It is important to express to parents when you are and aren't available to respond to them. This will help them manage their expectations and reduce anxiety when you are offline or unavailable. It is also important for you to regularly reach out to every family in your class, especially those who haven't made any contact with you in a while.

Chapter Six:

Testing Knowledge and

Grading Online

Grades carry a significant amount of weight for students. When they understand that their work is going to be assessed, they are motivated to learn. When assessments are performed well, students thrive and seek to better their learning experience. They know exactly what is expected of them and the goals they can aim for. Assessments give students set targets that help them reach new heights and acquire new skills. All of this helps students feel a sense of accomplishment, self-respect, and appreciation for their academic studies. However, when assessments are performed incorrectly students may become disengaged with school work or feel discouraged from absorbing new information. Poor assessments do not give students clear instructions about the expectations of the test, it's purpose, and how to complete it. When the assessment has been completed, teachers fail to give students constructive feedback on their performance or areas where they can improve in the future. The truth is that students genuinely care about how well they perform at school and one way to support them with their grades is to ensure that proper structures and systems are put in place in a virtual classroom that can maintain the same level of integrity in grading as traditional classrooms.

Online assessments require teachers to think differently about how to engage students through the learning material. The fact that teachers are not able to support students face-to-face means that students are compelled to take a greater level of responsibility when completing assessments. They don't have the luxury of signalling to their teacher for help during assessments or completing their assessment in an exam conducive environment. Instead, students need to cultivate a higher degree of self-discipline and monitor their own progress pertaining to school work and grades. Nevertheless, when online grading and assessments are administered effectively, they can boost the quality of testing available to students. Indeed, this is a win-win situation for both teacher and students. Online grading and assessment platforms can significantly improve the way teacher's offer information to their students. This ultimately would advance a teacher's teaching abilities as well as advance the students' learning capacity.

Through online grading and assessments, teachers can also improve upon their systems of storing, accessing, and tracking student performance. They can save, archive, or store student files online and track progress or easily identify patterns of learning. Teachers also don't need to worry about losing sheets of paper or compromising on a student's confidentiality when storing grades because all of the communication, results, and reports cannot disappear once they are responsibly stored online or on technological devices. Online grading and assessments also make it easier for teachers to guide students in their learning experience. Assessment apps or platforms with data analysis and reporting features can synthesize student data with a click of a button and teachers are able to draw better conclusions and see where more attention needs to be invested by the student. Lastly, students don't have to wait weeks or even months to receive feedback on their assessments because test results and reports are generated immediately after test data has been added. Furthermore, teachers can provide feedback in multiple ways including writing feedback in the learning management system, recording their voice, or creating a personal video message. Therefore it is clear to see that although setting up online grading and assessments can be an adjustment for both teacher and student, the opportunities and benefits of using this method are endless!

Methods for Effective Online Grading

I have emphasized throughout the book that to succeed in online teaching, planning in advance is imperative. This is also true when designing your online grading and assessment criteria. Teachers are expected to rethink traditional methods of designing assessments and start on a clean slate. New expectations need to be established, as well as a new mindset for assessing student performance. One of the best places to start when designing an online assessment is to ask yourself the following questions: What is my module intended to teach or develop in a student? How will students demonstrate that they have learned what was necessary to learn? What methods can I use to provide them with valuable feedback once the assessment has been completed? These questions will help you as the educator become more clear about your assessment requirements and how every assessment is connected to several learning outcomes. If you are not clear on what you are looking for, your students won't have the necessary guidance and support needed in completing class assessments.

Secondly, teachers need to know how online learning works before they can administer an online assessment. Before handing out a test, quiz, or assigning group projects, you must first experience what it feels like to be on the receiving-end. Take a quiz and assess the amount of time, level of difficulty, and possible skills that are required to complete it successfully. You can also interview students who have been taking online lessons for a while and ask them about their experience with taking online assessments. Understanding how your assessments will be received and the ways in which students will interact with them will also clarify the way you design your assessment instructions.

A lot of emphasis must be placed on enhancing the methods in which teachers communicate with students before, during, and after assessments. In a traditional classroom, a student who admits that they are confused about the requirements of the assessment won't raise any red flags about the quality of the assessment; however, in a virtual classroom the same scenario will. It can be useful to conduct an audit on your communication methods so that you are certain that your instructions are straight-forward and actionable. Remember that because your students cannot see you in person, they require more detail, examples, and explanations in several media formats to understand your expectations and what they are required to do in a test situation. Therefore, written instructions alone aren't enough. Instructions must be communicated in various formats such as through an infographic, diagram, image, video tutorial, and so forth.

Students who succeed in online learning and perform well in online assessments are mostly those who are self-disciplined. Many researchers in the past have found that a student's success in online learning is not necessarily due to their cognitive talents or technological skills. Rather, it has a lot to do with a student's non-cognitive strengths such as their ability to take responsibility for their work. Thus part of a teacher's responsibility in creating online assessments is to find ways of developing students' non-cognitive strengths and effectively communicating the importance of these skills or practices on a students' performance. This message can be conveyed through short exercises or activities at the beginning of a module or lesson that require students to develop a growth mindset, become more independent, and improve on their time management skills. It is true that students who can identify their own limitations can be better supported in learning healthier practices and skills. In cases where students are struggling to manage work or school demands on their own, teachers can incorporate lessons or modules strictly designed to build students' competencies with online learning.

Online teachers will also need methods for combatting cheating during online assessments. Teachers need to answer the question of how they will ensure that students are the ones who did the work (as opposed to their parents or peers). This is an important consideration to make because as children get smarter and learn how to use certain technologies, teachers are finding it more difficult to authenticate work and prevent cheating. It is becoming increasingly easy for students to find content online and copy and paste it as their own. Other students have even found tools to work their way around plagiarism detectors and submit work that is not originally theirs. Preventing cheating during assessments is perhaps a more manageable task for classroom teachers who can physically monitor students during test situations. Online teachers who are separated from their students by a computer screen do not have that luxury. Therefore, they need to find alternative ways of holding students accountable for the work that they produce. One way to do this is to administer random interim check-ins where the educator tests students on the spot or requires students to hand-in an assessment before the end of the lesson. These check-ins allow teachers to compare the quality of the work that students submit randomly to the quality of work they submit for grading. Any inconsistencies in the quality of work is worth investigating further to determine whether prepared assessments were completed by the student or not.

Another way of authenticating student's work is to design and personalize online assessments in a manner that makes it difficult for students to Google answers. Teachers can include questions that ask for the student's opinion or require the student to design their own images or diagrams. They can also conduct a Google search and see the kind of answers that pop up when assessment questions are typed in the search bar. Based on the search results, teachers can review how they ask the question, making them more unique in nature. Another suggestion is to require more creativity from students, asking them to draw on recent world events, personal experiences, or their own reflections. The greater the amount of imagination required, the harder it is for students to reproduce someone else's work. Teachers can also create assessments that require students to publicly share their task or activity with other learners or on public platforms. Students find it easier to cheat when their work will be submitted exclusively to the teacher. However, when their work is shared with others, the inclination to cheat is significantly reduced. This is because plagiarism is easier to detect when work is public and furthermore, on public platforms, students have their dignity to uphold.

With online assessments, teachers are also given the opportunity to incorporate students in the grading process. This allows collaboration with teachers and students that is hardly enforced in traditional classrooms. Online teachers can encourage their students to be co-creators in the classroom by monitoring and assessing their own progress. Not only will this improve student engagement but it will also empower students to set meaningful goals and assess their own performance during classes. Teachers can encourage self-assessment by making rubrics available on classroom portals, allowing students to set targets for every assessment, and identifying learning gaps.

Self-reflections can also be encouraged through creating a classroom blog or discussion board where students can share personal experiences grappling with the content and possible areas of improvement. While self-assessment is important, peer assessment is also a valuable tool for effective grading. Responsible peer assessment has the ability to strengthen the quality of feedback a student receives from their work and help them assess their progress. However, teachers need to be mindful that bad peer assessment that may be offensive in nature can have negative consequences to a student's learning experience. The goal therefore is to create a culture of compassion and unity among students and model the qualities of positive and uplifting feedback. Monitor all peer assessment exercises and reinforce the standards and protocols of effective communication throughout the process.

Best Ideas and Strategies for Testing Knowledge, Carrying Out Exams, and Grading Students Online

The topic of fairness comes up a lot when educators discuss strategies for administering online assessments. They want to be careful to offer students the same amount of transparency, value, and effective feedback that they received in a traditional classroom. Designing fair online assessments is possible when teachers determine the type of content they want to assess or the ways in which they want to present the assessment to their students. However before teachers can select the best online tools or media formats, they have to go through a checklist of questions to figure out what their assessment will include. Some of these questions include: how old are the students and how advanced should the assessment be? Will the assessment require free-response answers? Will the assessment require a series of multiple choice or true and false questions? Do you want a tool or platform that automatically grades students for you? Will some of the questions in the assessment require you to upload multimedia? Do you expect students to print the test and scan their completed document or fill in their answers online?

Once you have answered these questions, finding the right tools and designing sets of questions becomes easier. For example, if your assessment is for students in elementary school, you may consider a very user-friendly assessment software that includes a user tutorial. You may also want to include more multiple choice questions over free-responses to assess students' knowledge in a more simple way. Lastly, when assessing students in elementary school, you may want to add images or videos to explain instructions in a more engaging way as well as to ensure that your students understand what they are being graded on. Another consideration to make when designing your online assessments will be the time frame given to complete the assessment.

Since the students are not taking the test in one vicinity or at the same time, online teachers will need to be flexible with assessment deadlines. Some students who do not have access to technology may need to complete the test offline and find a way to submit it to their teacher through email or as a physical copy. Other students may have a network connection issue which may cause them to take longer to complete the assessment. In an exam situation where students are obligated to take the test at the same time, teachers must give their students time to plan all of their technological requirements well in advance. It may also be useful to offer students a sample test weeks before the exam so that they are familiar with the types of questions that will be asked and can therefore enter the exam more prepared.

To familiarize students with online assessments, teachers should create more opportunities for online testing. The more a teacher can assess their students online using multiple platforms and formats, the more comfortable students will be with taking online assessments. Exposing students to various online assessment tools is simply not enough. Teachers are expected to teach students on how to use these tools effectively so that students are able to provide valuable insights and responses in their tests. Assume that your students have no idea how to use any of the educational tools offered to them and dedicate a few lessons going over the format of various assessments and the multiple options available for giving a well-considered response. Perhaps it goes without saying but it is also just as important to teach students how to answer questions that you will incorporate in your assessments. For instance, if you decide to use mainly multiple-choice and short response questions, you would need to give them plenty of practice—through sample assessments—of how to offer quality responses.

It may also be useful to teach students how to read and follow instructions. As educators, we know how easily instructions are misinterpreted in a traditional classroom, however, when students are tasked to read instructions through a computer screen it can cause even more confusion. Plan lessons where you teach your students on strategies and skills to answer questions and follow instructions. You may have to literally model how to read instructions and the process of breaking down each sentence and soliciting valuable information. Some of the skills that you can teach students include how to read for understanding, how to reread a text for more clarity, the importance of being able to rephrase the question in a way that makes it simpler to understand, and how to determine how many facts or points a question is asking for. After each lesson, make a printable copy of what you taught available online so that students can have these tips and strategies available when taking online assessments.

There are also a number of tips and suggestions to follow for administering online exams and quizzes. Firstly, you can use platforms such as Zoom to host one-on-one oral exams and group exams when students are expected to take the test at the same time. Zoom will also allow you to save evidence of the exam on your personal technological device for your own review at a later time. To do this, simply activate the video recording function on your Zoom account. Another tip for administering online exams is to ensure that your assessment has included more synthesis questions that require students to offer creative insights and make it more difficult for them to cheat. It may also help to reduce student anxiety and stress going into the exam if you lowered the weighting of each exam on their overall grade. This would also allow students the opportunity to improve their grades over the course of several low-percentage exams or assessments.

For conducting self-assessments, you can use surveys and quizzes. The primary difference between surveys and quizzes is that surveys can be anonymous and are rarely graded. Thus they are more useful for obtaining student reflections on the content learned in class and their overall experience in the classroom. Quizzes on the other hand can be graded or linked to another assessment item. When administering peer assessment, create a universal rubric that students will use to grade their peers. Take time to go through the rubric and explain in length what it takes for a student to receive a particular scoring. Ensure that students know that their score is meant to positively help their peers continue to make good progress. You can also make the rubric available a few days before the peer assessment so that students have an opportunity to ask you any questions related to scoring.

You can also take the hassle out of administering assessments by using tools to make the online exam more secure and reduce the risk of cheating (for instance, there are options like Respondus Lockdown Browser and Monitor to help you authenticate assessments). Keep in mind however, that the more reliant you are on technology for security purposes, the higher the risk of failures and errors becomes. Hence, you can monitor specific parts of the exam and rely more on creative interpretation which makes it much more difficult to cheat. Moreover, students are less prone to cheat when they are given the necessary time to complete assessments. You can help your students with time management during assessments by using programs that provide sufficient warnings about remaining time, allowing students to plan their time accordingly. Some online quizzes will be scored automatically as soon as they're completed, letting students know how they've performed. If this isn't the case, let students know how much time you'll need to grade their work and always provide feedback in the form of comments on top of the grade.

Three Assessment Concerns and Solutions

Effective online assessments are those that are adapted to the online learning environment. It can be tempting for teachers to recycle questions and testing formats that worked well in a traditional classroom setting, however this is not always a good idea. Since the method of presenting and administering online assessments is different than those used in traditional assessments, teachers must learn to tweak or completely replace their previous assessment framework. Tweaking your assessments is important due to the following five concerns that are presented when assessing students online. Firstly, online students require more interaction with the educator than students who have face-to-face access. This interaction, when carefully planned, can help online students grasp the content more efficiently and help them feel more supported in their learning. Some of the ways that you can strengthen the interaction with your students is by offering regular, low-stake assessments and activities such as short quizzes, to help students take action with the information they learn in class.

Another way to strengthen interaction with your students is to provide quality and in-depth feedback for every activity or assessment completed in the module. You can simply add detailed feedback to quiz responses, leave them under student posts on the classroom discussion board, or incorporate weekly surveys that ask students to identify concepts that they are finding challenging in class. After receiving the survey feedback, create quick clarifying videos explaining these challenging concepts with greater detail and offering more practical examples. The second concern with regards to setting up online assessments is that students require more planned structure when carrying out tests. They require more assistance and support with staying on time and on task with every activity. For example, seeing the words "test next Wednesday" on a classroom chalkboard would be sufficient enough to remind students to prepare for their test. However, in a virtual classroom, more instructions and planning is needed. A great solution to provide your students with more structure is to break up large projects into smaller tasks and activities that can be graded.

Doing this would help students keep up with the demands of class work and make it easier for misunderstandings to be clarified earlier on. Grading each milestone will also provide students with a number of opportunities to improve on their grades and performance in class. The third concern with regards to online assessments is that presentations or demonstrations can be more difficult to administer successfully online. Students may have found it easier to give a face-to-face classroom speech or presentation because they had the support of their peers. During online learning, students are required to complete presentations without making comparisons with their fellow classmates' work. They also have the enormous task of packaging their presentation in a way that provides the teacher with enough evidence that they have understood the requirements of the activity. Teachers can support students with delivering graded presentations by offering them numerous video creation and editing softwares to choose from and tutorials on how to maximize on the features of each one. Students can also be encouraged to start threads on the classroom discussion board or set up group video calls with other classmates to discuss ideas for presentations and share valuable tips.

Chapter Seven:

Maintaining the Relationship Between Student and Teacher in the Digital Classroom

The student-teacher relationship should be at the core of all learning management plans whether classes are held in traditional classrooms or online. This relationship forms the foundation for all classroom engagements between students and the teachers, and facilitates all classroom activities. Teachers who do not invest time and effort in strengthening or maintaining this relationship will soon experience an emotional disconnect with students, influencing the learning environment in the classroom. Students become "difficult" or display signs of apathy or resistance to learning when they don't feel understood or heard by their teacher. Once a relationship has been formed, teachers are able to get through to difficult students and learn of ways to help them excel in class and how to relate to them better. Without forming a healthy relationship, there will always be a barrier between the teacher and the student.

Online teaching, with its many technologies, provides countless opportunities for teachers to engage with students in a more relatable and natural way. Online tools can be used by teachers to engage with students more efficiently and using channels that are more familiar with students. However, the inherent efficiency of using online technologies could also cause teachers to neglect maintaining their relationship with students and use these tools as barriers. For example, a teacher could design a video once and present it to groups of students every time they enter a new class. Eventually, authentic interaction with the teacher is replaced with a video, slideshow, or voice recording. When technology is used as a barrier between students and teachers, the learning experience becomes repetitive and thus predictable. Students start to feel alone on their learning journey and over time become disinterested or lose the emotional connection to the course or subject they are studying.

For many online teachers, the question of how to build relationships with online students has been an ongoing one. Whether you are teaching a short course, tutoring students online, or facilitating distance learning, your ability to connect with students is the make-or-break factor to effective online teaching. Online teachers seek to recreate the vibrant energy that one would find in a traditional classroom through a computer screen. Sounds tough, right? Well, the truth is it isn't. The key to building relationships with your online students is simple: be present. One of the most recorded concerns that students have with the online learning process is the lack of instructor presence in the virtual classroom. Many times students feel as though they are being taught by a computer screen rather than a real teacher. It is ironic that many online teachers aren't quite clear on ways to show up for their students online. They assume that students will work through the learning material and administer tests on their own without a lot of intervention from them.

Online students prioritize the relationship with their online teacher because it is the only authentic academic relationship they can have that can help them succeed in their course or understand the content better. Students want to know that there is somebody who cares about their class performance on the other side of the screen. They want to feel as though they are in a strong partnership with the teacher and that support is available whenever it is required. Therefore, strategies to establish and maintain this one-of-a-kind relationship must be studied by teachers and implemented during online interactions.

Practical Strategies for Establishing Relationship With Students Online

There are several simple and straightforward strategies that teachers can implement in their virtual classrooms to establish relationships with students. Fortunately, technological tools can assist teachers in bridging the social gap between themselves and students and help in cultivating a healthy relationship. The first practical strategy is for teachers to use technological tools to design instructor-created video content. These videos are particularly useful in asynchronous courses or lessons where the teacher is not available to walk the student through the class or course. These videos only need to be recorded once for every lesson or course and added in each session to establish the presence of the teacher in that session. Even though these pre-recorded videos are not new, students feel as though the teacher made an effort to guide their learning experience every step of the way. Ideas of content for your instructor-created videos include making a video detailing course expectations, assigning tutorials, or recapping on the core themes and ideas learned in each lesson.

The second practical strategy for building relationships with students is to create a video biography. Creating a video biography is quick and easy, plus the benefits of producing such highly personalized content are manifold. Video biographies are simply videos where teachers introduce themselves and welcome students to the class. During these videos, teachers can share as much or as little about themselves as they desire, however, students value hearing about a teacher's background and the experience they bring into the classroom. These videos are valuable assets for your online modules or lessons because they will help you as the educator gain a level of credibility from your students. Generally, if you present yourself as an expert in your subject or as someone who is passionate about what they teach, students will feel more compelled to engage with the lesson content and complete all class activities. When sharing information about yourself in these videos, don't focus solely on your academic achievements or listing the colleges you attended. Instead, include topics such as your hobbies, favorite foods, or favorite music genre. These topics help students find commonalities between the two of you and establish a bond immediately.

The third practical strategy for building a strong relationship with students is to share relevant personal experiences. When teachers incorporate stories in lessons, they can help students draw connections between the content and real-life scenarios or events. These experiences don't necessarily have to be the teachers' personal account. They can include relevant case studies or recent developments in world events. Regardless of the format of the story, it is important to use a storytelling tone of voice when doing so. This will allow students to activate their imaginations and immerse themselves in this personal experience. Sharing these personal stories will help teachers build credibility in the classroom and earn extra points for sharing intriguing stories. Teachers can share personal experiences through text, pre-recorded videos, or in real-time video conferencing. The most important point to remember when sharing these accounts is to keep them relevant. Share stories that will help students understand how to practically apply the content of the lesson in their personal life experiences.

The fourth and final strategy for establishing relationships with students is to show interest in their lives. Taking an interest in a student's life is easier when school takes place in a physical building where the teacher can meet with the student face-to-face and engage on a personal level. The convenience of online teaching can sometimes cause teachers to focus on delivering innovative content but forget about the importance of getting to know students on a deeper level. Online students require more support and interaction from their teachers than those who attend traditional school. When online students notice their teacher taking interest in their lives, they are motivated to make steady progress in their school work. The validation and acknowledgement that students receive from teachers simply setting up a meeting for a one-on-one check-in can go a long way in building a solid relationship between the teacher and student. It is also just as important for teachers to create opportunities for students to share their lives with their peers and receive support from a community of students. One of the ways that teachers can initiate a deeper connection with students is by asking them questions. Asking questions is a clear and simple sign that shows students that the teacher is paying attention. Some questions that are posed to questions can be useful in making sure they understand class requirements, however, teachers should also ask random and fun questions such as: what is your dream destination? Or what is your favorite dessert?

Cultivating a Strong Community in a Virtual Classroom

One of my good friends, an English teacher, was asked to conduct an online English course geared toward highschool learners. Unfortunately, many of her students had already dropped out of the online course by midterm and the course had to be cancelled. When I sat down with her and asked what happened, my friend told me that the class failed because she began teaching the course without properly establishing a strong community. She assumed that since it was an English course, the students were only interested in learning about the subject. What she didn't recognize is by establishing a strong community, her students would have enjoyed the experience of learning English better. In a traditional classroom, there are so many verbal and non-verbal practices that allow students to cultivate a community in their classroom. These same practices are rarely translated effectively in virtual classrooms. Creating a community in a virtual classroom requires a different set of strategies that are predominantly based on cultivating trust, respect, and responsibility between student relationships and the student-teacher relationship.

The first step that you can take in cultivating a community in your online class is to complete a culture inventory. For those teachers who have already begun teaching online, you can identify the existing culture in your online class and ask yourself the following questions: Do your students show up to class for live video sessions? Are your students interacting with the learning material in the way you hoped for? Do your students' work reflect the learning outcomes you had set for the class? Are your students communicating with you on a regular and consistent basis? If your responses to these questions are all positive, you can continue doing what you are doing; in contrast, if these questions prove that the focus in your classroom is not on learning, you have an opportunity to create a classroom culture that will help students actively participate in class and engage more with the content. If on the other hand your course or online lessons haven't begun, you can use the questions above as a reference to the kind of culture you hope to create in your classroom. Keep the vision of the kind of culture you seek to cultivate in your classroom when drafting your lesson plans and preparing your online toolbox. This vision will become a source of inspiration you can always draw from.

The second step is to establish digital community agreements with your students. These agreements will be made during the introductory stage of your lesson or course. It is important that you make these agreements during a live synchronous experience where students can engage with you directly and ask questions. These agreements will help you as the teacher receive consent from your students on how virtual interactions between peers and the teacher will be undertaken. It is important to revisit these agreements frequently so that students are reminded of the expectations and culture within the classroom setting. For instance, you can spend the first five minutes of a live class to play a game of popcorn where the students can take turns shouting out the agreements. This game should be fun, quick, but significant enough to remind students of their expected conduct and behavior during the class.

The third step is to establish trusting relationships. Trust in a virtual classroom is cultivated through forging relationships with students as well as through helping students cultivate empathy and understanding for each other. Trust is built through every online interaction, whether it takes place in real-time or through various online channels. For example, trust can be built from the teachers responsiveness to emails received from students and parents or by being available during the office hours that were communicated. Trust is also built through every announcement made by the teacher, as well as in every detailed feedback given to students. Teachers can also earn trust by putting themselves in the student's shoes and making executive decisions that are considerate to the needs and experiences of students. For example, teachers must make sure that every student has the necessary device or access to the same platform before teaching can begin. They need to personally check-in with each student to make sure that they know how to turn on the mic, webcam, or make use of every feature available on the learning platform.

The fourth step is to build respect. This step becomes easier once a foundation of trust has been built. The best way to earn and show students respect is to get to know each student personally and accommodate their learning needs in every lesson. A simple way to get to know students is by assigning them a survey to complete at the beginning of a class that will ask them to share interesting and personal information about themselves. Students are not obligated to answer questions that may be too personal to reveal or make them feel uncomfortable in any way. Instead, encourage them to share as much information as they desire. Your response to the surveys will be a lesson where you introduce yourself as the teacher and share interesting information about your teaching experiences. You can also open the floor for students to ask you questions about your personal life in order for them to get to know you better. You are not obligated to reveal everything about yourself and it is okay to notify students on topics that are off limits.

Once you are familiar with the students and they are familiar with you, it becomes easier to speak openly about classroom boundaries and behavior that is unacceptable. Students understand the difference between disruptive and productive behavior and after mutual respect is built, they will help you ensure that boundaries and classroom rules and standards are maintained. Another way of earning respect from students is to collaborate with them on ideas for future activities and projects. Acknowledge their ideas by incorporating them in the lesson plans and notice how engaged the students become in class. Every once in a while, ask students how they are feeling about the pace of the class and whether they would like to incorporate new online tools during lessons. Use as many student suggestions as you can while maintaining the integrity of the lesson. You can also assign students various roles during classes like the note-taker, time-keeper, and class-monitor whose responsibility is to help the teacher regulate the virtual classroom. Select different students in each lesson to assume the various roles and maintain a culture of collaboration in your class.

The fifth and final step for cultivating a strong community in your virtual classroom is to give your students responsibility over their learning experience. The expectation that the teacher is responsible for spoon-feeding students information while they sit back and take it all in will not build a strong community. Students need to be taught how to regulate their own emotions, manage their time constructively, and focus attentively in class. The more responsible each community member is, the better the flow of lessons will be. Teachers can include a lesson every week where the topic is related to an aspect of self-development. In these lessons, students will learn how to manage their time, cope with stress, ask for help, and achieve a balance between home and school life. Teachers can also help students create a functioning daily routine that offers them an opportunity to work and play. Teachers can also introduce students to online tools that will help them organize their calendars and set reminders for upcoming commitments.

When practiced continuously, these five steps will help you create a virtual classroom environment where students feel comfortable engaging in lessons and enjoying every minute of it. They will also help you become an active listener and genuinely taek interest in the welfare of your students. The more you invest in the student-teacher relationship, the greater your returns will be. Students will notice your openness and presence in each lesson and raise their standards to give you the same respect and presence in return. At the end of the day, establishing or maintaining the student-teacher relationship is a win-win for both parties involved and ensures that the knowledge from lessons is transferred with ease.

Conclusion

Talks of how technology would revolutionize education have been in circulation for many decades. Many research studies have predicted the involvement and to some degree, take-over of technology in the traditional classroom. The inclusion of technology in various parts of a students learning experience happened gradually. At first the classroom overhead projector was replaced with a smartboard and then in recent years, workbooks were replaced with tablet devices. Nevertheless, with all of these changes taking place right before our eyes, none of us could have predicted the sudden migration to online learning that would take place in the space of a few months, spurred by an unexpected global pandemic. With schools closing indefinitely and teachers having to figure out ways of continuing to engage with their students, strategies for online teaching have become invaluable.

Many teachers who branched out into online teaching would have noticed the vast differences between the traditional and virtual classroom. To compare the two would be the same as comparing apples and pears. Online learning, as many teachers would have found, requires a particular mindset to achieve optimum results. Teachers cannot rely on their years of experience or the rigorous training they received on how to manage students in a traditional classroom. Instead, they are forced to think laterally about the many possibilities available to them online to teach existing concepts and ideas in new and engaging ways. The teachers who thrive in online learning are those who are flexible enough to adapt to new technologies and experiment with various online tools in the classroom. They are aware that the pace at which technology is evolving is similar to the pace at which students' personal lives are evolving too, thus it is important that students are exposed to new information, trends, tools, and insights to enrich their educational experience.

Perhaps the selling point for online learning can be summarized in one word: value. The only way teachers can make online learning worthwhile is if it offers students a more valuable experience than traditional learning. This implies that online classes should incorporate cutting-edge technologies that allow students to be at the forefront of the change taking place in our world. Instead of structuring lessons in a lecture-style, teachers need to make better use of their time by providing students with opportunities to be creative, discover new ideas, and collaborate with other learners. This forward-thinking manner of teaching also implies that students are no longer passive observers in the classroom. They share the platform with the teacher as co-creators and enjoy the privilege of shaping their learning experience through sharing knowledge with their class. Virtual classrooms become valuable when students can take a concept presented by the teacher and peel off its layers until the core message or theme is exposed. Valuable lessons are those where the teacher takes mindful breaks to assess how well the students are responding to the content through playing a game or allowing students to breakout into small groups for a mini discussion. Instead of placing emphasis on running through all of the slides, teachers focus on quality in which information is delivered to students.

The end-goal of online learning is not to secure a one-hundred percent pass rate or secure an impressive class average. Rather, the end-goal is to prepare students to cope with the ever-changing environment around them. The future will be full of unexpected twists and turns similar to the one we experienced in the beginning of this decade. The role of teachers therefore is to prepare a generation of leaders, thinkers, strategists, and innovators who will have the necessary skills and tools to solve new problems, cope with new challenges, and employ new technologies. When virtual classrooms are run successfully, they offer online students the necessary training to handle both the challenges and opportunities available in their environment. From this perspective, you can see how indispensable the role of the online teacher is in grooming students to become influential in their communities. Online teachers also have the responsibility to curate a unique learning experience where students are able to maintain a high level of engagement with the content and apply the knowledge that they gain in their personal lives.

My intention for writing this book was to respond to a global cry for resources and techniques when teaching students online. The strategies and tips that you have acquired throughout the book will position you for success in your online teaching journey. Of course, you will make mistakes along the way, but choose to see those mistakes as necessary learning curves. I have found that every mistake I made during my first year of online teaching led me to a new online tool or gave me an opportunity to learn about a new feature on a platform. As you navigate your way into online teaching, adopt a level of curiosity that will give you the confidence to sample apps and tools that are out of your comfort zone. Add a touch of spontaneity to your lessons and consider what your students would find entertaining or interesting to learn. While there are clear-cut methods for designing lesson plans or assessments, there are no clear-cut formulas in presenting engaging lessons to your students. Therefore, you have the liberty to pick and choose the various tips and tricks that work for you and the kind of culture you seek to establish in your virtual classroom.

You can now rest assured that you have all of the ingredients to establish and operate a successful virtual classroom. Remember that you are an asset to your students and the more you open yourself up to the online learning experience, the more enriching your classes will be. Since you have the freedom to present information to your students in your own special way, make sure that you include a touch of your own personality as well as those of your students in all that you do. In this way, teaching will become yet another outlet for you to share who you are with your students and for them to share who they are with you! Oh how wonderful it is to think that learning can become so integrated with real-life.

References

Best, J. (2020, March 12). *5 challenges of online teaching (and how to rise above them).* 3P Learning. https://www.3plearning.com/blog/5-common-pitfalls-distance-teaching-avoid/

Bindel, A. (2019a, February). *Spiral review for teachers.* Common Sense Education. https://www.commonsense.org/education/website/spiral

Bindel, A. (2019b, March 21). *Bloomz.* Common Sense Education. https://www.commonsense.org/education/app/bloomz

Blades, N. (2015, November 2). *SimplyCircle app streamlines parent-school communication.* Cool Mom Tech. https://coolmomtech.com/2015/11/simplycircle-app-review-parent-school-commmunications/

Braddock, P. (2020, May 6). *How to prepare teachers to teach online.* Www.Britishcouncil.Org. https://www.britishcouncil.org/voices-magazine/prepare-teachers-online-lessons

Briggs, A. (2015, February 11). *Ten ways to overcome barriers to student engagement online (Academic technology: At the college of William and Mary).* OLC. https://onlinelearningconsortium.org/news_ite m/ten-ways-overcome-barriers-student-engagement-online/

Caudill, A. (2018, December 27). *Color-coding: The differentiation strategy you never knew you needed.* WeAreTeachers. https://www.weareteachers.com/color-coding-classroom/

Chalk. (n.d.). *Chalk support - Planboard guide - Chapter 2: Lesson planning.* Help.Chalk.Com. Retrieved September 20, 2020, from https://help.chalk.com/learning-guides/planboard-guide/planboard-chapter-two

Commonsense. (2013, November 16). *TES teach with blendspace review for teachers.* Common Sense Education. https://www.commonsense.org/education/we bsite/tes-teach-with-blendspace#:~:text=TES%20Teach%20with% 20Blendspace%20is

Commonsense. (2016, May 10). *Planboard review for teachers.* Common Sense Education. https://www.commonsense.org/education/we bsite/planboard

Conway, P. (2013, October 8). *Skype review for teachers.* Common Sense Education. https://www.commonsense.org/education/we bsite/skype#:~:text=Pros%3A%20It

David, G. (n.d.). *Alignment principle of Ddsign*. Graphic Design Services In Kenya. Retrieved September 20, 2020, from https://254-online.com/alignment-principle-design/

Denby, J. (2020, July). *ReadTheory review for teachers*. Common Sense Education. https://www.commonsense.org/education/website/readtheory

Dimeo, J. (2017, November 15). *Peer advice for instructors teaching online for first time*. Www.Insidehighered.Com. https://www.insidehighered.com/digital-learning/article/2017/11/15/peer-advice-instructors-teaching-online-first-time

EdSurge. (n.d.). *Common curriculum - Product reviews*. Retrieved September 20, 2020, from https://www.edsurge.com/product-reviews/common-curriculum

Findley, J. (2017, March 5). *Online testing strategies: Prepare your students to take online assessments*. Teaching with Jennifer Findley. https://jenniferfindley.com/online-testing-strategies/

Garcia-Bulle, S. (2019, May 17). *The excess of content and the decreasing attention span in students*. Observatory of Educational Innovation. https://observatory.tec.mx/edu-news/attention-span-students

Grove, J. V. (2011, March 5). *Projeqt is an online storytelling engine for creatives [INVITES].* Mashable. https://mashable.com/2011/03/04/projeqt/

Gutierrez, K. (2014, January 30). *The eLearning dilemma: Engaged vs unengaged learners.* Www.Shiftelearning.Com. https://www.shiftelearning.com/blog/bid/334167/The-eLearning-Dilemma-Engaged-vs-Unengaged-Learners

Hale, J., Grenny, J., & Swedberg, L. (2020, March 17). *How to get people (Students) to actually participate in virtual meetings (Classes).* Hbsp.Harvard.Edu. https://hbsp.harvard.edu/inspiring-minds/how-to-get-people-students-to-actually-participate-in-virtual-meetings-classes

Henry, L. (2020, May 1). *Fostering a strong community in a virtual classroom.* Edutopia. https://www.edutopia.org/article/fostering-strong-community-virtual-classroom

Jansen, K. (2019, May 16). *30 useful communication apps for your school.* BookWidgets Blog. https://www.bookwidgets.com/blog/2019/05/30-useful-communication-apps-for-your-school

Johnson, S. (2020, March 25). *Developing online assessments of student learning in a hurry.* Vanderbilt University. https://www.vanderbilt.edu/brightspace/2020/03/25/developing-online-assessments-of-student-learning-in-a-hurry-we-have-resources-for-you/

Katz, N. (2020, May 12). *Tips and tools for giving online assessments to students.* WeAreTeachers. https://www.weareteachers.com/online-assessments/

Kelleher, I., & Hulleman, C. (2020, August 21). *The science of keeping kids engaged—Even from home.* Edutopia. https://www.edutopia.org/article/science-keeping-kids-engaged-even-home

Kent, D. (2020, April 29). *How Cisco Webex transforms your distance learning schedule.* Mio Dispatch. https://dispatch.m.io/cisco-webex-distance-learning-schedule/

Kumar, S. (2015, July 10). *5 common problems faced by students in eLearning and how to overcome them.* ELearning Industry. https://elearningindustry.com/5-common-problems-faced-by-students-in-elearning-overcome

Lambert, E. (2017). *myHomework student planner review for teachers.* Common Sense Education. https://www.commonsense.org/education/app/myhomework-student-planner

Learn how to transform your face-to-face classes into online classes. (2020, April 29). BlogCoursify.Me. https://blog.coursify.me/en/how-to-create-online-classes/

Leicester Learning Institute. (n.d.). *Writing and structuring online learning materials.* Retrieved September 19,

2020, from https://www2.le.ac.uk/offices/lli/case-studies-and-resources/repository/learning-and-teaching-resources/writing-and-structuring-online-learning-materials-pdf

Martin, J. (2019). Building relationships and increasing engagement in the virtual classroom. *The Journal of Educators Online*, *16*(1). https://doi.org/10.9743/jeo.2019.16.1.9

Martin, J. E. (n.d.). *Grading and assessing online student work: Core concepts and key strategies you can use today.* Blackbaud Inc. Retrieved September 26, 2020, from https://hello.blackbaud.com/rs/053-MXJ-131/images/11043_JonathanMartin_eBook.pdf

Microsoft. (n.d.). *Distance learning with Microsoft Teams for education.* Retrieved September 22, 2020, from https://cczv.cuni.cz/CCZV-220-version1-ppt_ms_aj.pdf

Millsaps, J. (2018, June 1). *How to work with different personalities in your classroom.* Https://Blog.Alo7.Com/. https://blog.alo7.com/work-different-personalities-classroom/

Minero, E. (2020, August 21). *8 strategies to improve participation in your virtual classroom.* Edutopia. https://www.edutopia.org/article/8-strategies-improve-participation-your-virtual-classroom

MobileMind. (2020, June 9). *Distance learning essentials: Google hangouts meet.* MobileMind. https://mobilemind.io/distance-learning-essentials-google-hangouts-meet/

Moore, E. A. (2013, December 2). *7 assessment challenges of moving your course online (Plus solutions).* Faculty Focus. https://www.facultyfocus.com/articles/online-education/7-assessment-challenges-of-moving-your-course-online-solutions/

Morin, A. (n.d.). *5 reasons students aren't engaging in distance learning.* Www.Understood.Org. Retrieved September 23, 2020, from https://www.understood.org/en/school-learning/for-educators/empathy/5-reasons-students-arent-engaging-in-distance-learning

Morrison, D. (2013). 10 reasons students don't participate in online discussions how to remedy each. In *Online Learning Insights.* https://onlinelearninginsights.files.wordpress.com/2013/10/online_dicussions_facilitator_resource.pdf

Narcisi, G. (2020, September 1). *Cisco Webex classrooms unveiled for education-focused partners.* CRN. https://www.crn.com/news/networking/cisco-webex-classrooms-unveiled-for-education-focused-partners

Ovcharova, M. (2019, January 13). *How to plan a virtual classroom lesson.* VEDAMO.

https://www.vedamo.com/knowledge/plan-virtual-classroom-lesson/

Pascale F.M. (2020, March 29). *Rhymezone is rated "Average" with 3.7 / 5 on Trustpilot*. Trustpilot. https://www.trustpilot.com/review/rhymezone.com

Phillips, J. (2016, October 20). *7 tips on how to prepare for teaching online*. ELearning Industry. https://elearningindustry.com/7-tips-prepare-for-teaching-online

Powers, M. (2018, November 26). *Flipgrid*. Common Sense Education. https://www.commonsense.org/education/website/flipgrid

Rae, N. (2020, February 17). *How to plan an online teaching lesson (With examples)*. Goats On The Road. https://www.goatsontheroad.com/online-teaching-lesson-plan/#Components_of_a_Good_Online_Teaching_Lesson_Plan

Raz-Kids review for teachers. (2013, May 7). Common Sense Education. https://www.commonsense.org/education/website/raz-kids

Rogowski, M. (2013, April 26). *Socrative review for teachers*. Common Sense Education. https://www.commonsense.org/education/website/socrative

Rogowski, M. (2015, April 9). *Formative review for teachers.* Common Sense Education. https://www.commonsense.org/education/we bsite/formative

Rogowski, M. (2018a, March). *ParentSquare review for teachers.* Common Sense Education. https://www.commonsense.org/education/we bsite/parentsquare

Rogowski, M. (2018b, October). *Edpuzzle.* Common Sense Education. https://www.commonsense.org/education/we bsite/edpuzzle

Rogowski, M. (2018c, October 25). *Seesaw: The learning journal.* Common Sense Education. https://www.commonsense.org/education/app /seesaw-the-learning-journal

Rogowski, M. (2018d, November). *Remind review for teachers.* Common Sense Education. https://www.commonsense.org/education/we bsite/remind

Rogowski, M. (2018e, December 11). *ClassDojo.* Common Sense Education. https://www.commonsense.org/education/we bsite/classdojo

Rogowski, M. (2020, April). *Edmodo review for teachers.* Common Sense Education. https://www.commonsense.org/education/we bsite/edmodo

Schoch, K. (2015, March 14). *Testmoz.* Techtoolsforassessment.Pbworks.Com. http://techtoolsforassessment.pbworks.com/w/page/93436025/Testmoz

Sitkin, J. (2014, June 19). *Engrade review for teachers.* Common Sense Education. https://www.commonsense.org/education/website/engrade

Starkey, H. (2020, March 27). *True education partnerships.* True Education Partnerships. https://www.trueeducationpartnerships.com/schools/20-of-the-best-online-teacher-communities/

TeachAde - Free educational resources for educators and teachers. (n.d.). Www.Teachade.Com. Retrieved September 19, 2020, from http://www.teachade.com/

Team TpT. (2020, March 27). *Distance learning: Tips for supporting parents and families.* The TpT Blog. https://blog.teacherspayteachers.com/distance-learning-tips-for-supporting-parents-and-families/

ThingLink review for teachers. (2014, March 25). Common Sense Education. https://www.commonsense.org/education/website/thinglink

Trach, E. (2019, April 5). *7 Best presentation tools for students.* Www.Schoology.Com.

https://www.schoology.com/blog/7-best-presentation-tools-students

Tutor Doctor. (n.d.). *Problems and solutions for distance learning.* Tutor Doctor. Retrieved September 18, 2020, from https://www.tutordoctor.com/blog/2015/may/problems-and-solutions-for-distance-learning/

Vander Borght, M. (2012, June 19). *Storybird review for teachers.* Common Sense Education. https://www.commonsense.org/education/website/storybird

Wilkey, E. (2020, April 27). *Teachers' essential guide to Zoom.* Common Sense Education. https://www.commonsense.org/education/articles/teachers-essential-guide-to-zoom

Made in the USA
Middletown, DE
24 January 2021